THE EVERYTHING

ESSENTIAL SPANISH BOOK

Dear Reader,

I know learning a new language isn't easy—I, too, have had to start from the beginning and learn a language that I now call my own. It took a lot of effort on my part, but it was also a great deal of fun. It took me places that I never expected.

Whatever your reason for learning Spanish, I'm glad you're getting started. Today, Spanish is one of the most widely spoken languages in the world. Just think—Spanish-language speakers are everywhere, from Argentina to Puerto Rico to Spain to the United States. By learning just one language, you can tap into so many cultures!

This book is meant to guide you through the most important parts of the Spanish language. As you go through each essential chapter, keep chipping away at memorizing vocabulary words and practicing Spanish grammar. And don't forget to try and practice what you're learning. It's the only way to really be able to hold on to it.

Good luck!

Julie Gutin

Welcome to the EVERYTHING Series!

These handy, accessible books give you all you need to tackle a difficult project, gain a new hobby, or even brush up on something you learned back in school but have since forgotten. You can choose to read from cover to cover or just pick out information from our four useful boxes.

 Alerts

Urgent warnings

 Facts

Important snippets of information

 **Essentials**

Quick handy tips

 **Questions**

Answers to common questions

When you're done reading, you can finally say you know **EVERYTHING®**!

PUBLISHER Karen Cooper

MANAGING EDITOR, EVERYTHING® SERIES Lisa Laing

COPY CHIEF Casey Ebert

ASSOCIATE PRODUCTION EDITOR Mary Beth Dolan

ACQUISITIONS EDITOR Eileen Mullan

DEVELOPMENT EDITOR Eileen Mullan

EVERYTHING® SERIES COVER DESIGNER Erin Alexander

Visit the entire Everything® series at *www.everything.com*

THE
EVERYTHING®
ESSENTIAL
SPANISH BOOK

All you need to learn Spanish in no time

Julie Gutin

Technical Review by Fernanda Ferreira, PhD

A adamsmedia

Avon, Massachusetts

An Everything® Series Book.
Everything® and everything.com® are registered trademarks of F+W Media, Inc.

Published by Adams Media, a division of F+W Media, Inc.
57 Littlefield Street, Avon, MA 02322. U.S.A.
www.adamsmedia.com

Contains material adapted and abridged from *The Everything® Learning Spanish Book, 2nd Edition* by Julie Gutin, copyright © 2007 by F+W Media, Inc., ISBN 10: 1-59869-173-2, ISBN 13: 978-1-59869-173-3.

ISBN 10: 1-4405-6621-6
ISBN 13: 978-1-4405-6621-9
eISBN 10: 1-4405-6622-4
eISBN 13: 978-1-4405-6622-6

Printed in the United States of America.

10   9   8   7   6   5   4   3   2   1

This book is available at quantity discounts for bulk purchases.
For information, please call 1-800-289-0963.

Contents

Introduction

Welcome to *The Everything® Essential Spanish Book* and the exciting and diverse world of the Spanish language! Maybe you chose to pick up this book because you want to be able to communicate with some of your Spanish-speaking coworkers, neighbors, or clients. Perhaps you want to feel more comfortable traveling in countries where Spanish is the national language. Maybe you just want to brush up on what you learned in your high school Spanish class. Whatever your reasons for learning this popular language, you've come to the right place.

While it might seem like a daunting task to take on learning a new language, just imagine the sense of accomplishment you will feel when you find yourself in Mexico City and need to ask for directions, and you approach the first person you see and say confidently, *"¡Perdón! ¿Dónde está la calle San José?"* (Excuse me, where is San Jose Street?). And imagine your feelings when the person answers in Spanish and you are able to understand the directions!

Learning the Spanish essentials will expand your intellectual horizons. You will be in a position to learn about Hispanic cultures from the inside—by listening to Latin music, reading books in Spanish, and conversing with native speakers. You will have more personal opportunities to witness how other people live day by day in your own neighborhood, on their own terms. Not only will you be able to listen to their opinions on family, life, work, and society in general, but you will be able to come to a mutual understanding by sharing your own.

Knowing basic Spanish might even help you in your career. Given the trend toward globalization, you will not only be able to take advantage of many opportunities that already exist, but that you currently know nothing about. The business opportunities are obvious—a larger market for sales or employment.

Learning any new language can be a difficult undertaking, but if you persevere, the results will be worth your effort. And there's more good news—Spanish isn't as foreign a language as you might think. Take a quick look at the chapters of this book. I'm sure you'll recognize a few words or phrases here and there. If you ever studied Spanish or another Romance language, something did stick, even if you don't realize it. Even if you've never studied a foreign language before, you'll discover that you already know a few things. Don't worry if you are starting from scratch. You'll see that even those years of studying English grammar will be helpful.

Whatever your interests are in learning Spanish, this book will help you achieve the goals that you have set for yourself. *Buena suerte* (good luck) in your endeavor!

CHAPTER 1

Starting with the Basics

B efore you begin reading this book, it is important to remember that learning a new language should always be enjoyable. Of course you'll need to dedicate a certain amount of time and attention in order for you to make progress, but above all, this endeavor should be fun and stress-free!

Developing Basic Language Skills

If you are full of enthusiasm to sit down and learn *español* (Spanish) at one go—*¡relájate!*—stop and relax. Learning a language is not like crash dieting; it's a gradual process that requires planning and concentration. Here is what you should know as you incorporate learning Spanish into your everyday life.

Things to Remember
Avoid negative thinking—that you can never master a foreign language, or that it's impossible for you to pronounce certain words correctly. Relax, and concentrate on what you do know and *can* do, and then keep adding on to that. If you can't think of a particular word, choose another one to help you explain yourself. If you can't understand what someone is saying to you, ask him to repeat.

The expressive potential of a sentence is often more than the sum of its parts. Don't just concentrate on memorizing words—you also need to know how to put these words together to make meaningful statements. Learning whole phrases will help you make your point quicker.

 Alert

To really have Spanish vocabulary available to you at your fingertips, invest in an English-to-Spanish and Spanish-to-English dictionary. Choose the one that best suits you, the one you will have completely dog-eared within a month.

Use new phrases as soon as you have learned them and as many times as possible. Don't wait until you have everything down perfectly before you begin using Spanish in conversation. When it comes to languages, perfect fluency and pronunciation are myths. Your goal should be to get out there and start talking as soon as possible.

Get online. You're just a click of a mouse away from finding free instruction, opportunities to practice, reference materials, and cultural information, as well as online Spanish courses.

Immerse yourself in the world of Spanish. Eat at Spanish and Latin American restaurants. Listen to music from Spanish-speaking countries: *boleros, cumbias, flamenco, merengue, pasillos, pasodoble, salsas, sevillanas, el son, tango, rancheras,* and *rock.* Go out to Latin dance clubs. Seek out movies in Spanish playing at international film festivals, and rent Spanish films on video or DVD—most will offer subtitles or dubbed tracks in Spanish. Read bilingual books and magazines. Try watching Spanish television—at first you won't understand it, but it might be fun to guess what is happening.

 Fact

There are at least four major Spanish-language networks available in the United States: *Galavisión* (cable), *TeleFutura, Telemundo,* and *Univision.* Check your local listings for these and other offerings.

Combine your hobbies and interests with the study of Spanish. If you love playing tennis, learn how to say everything you know about the game in Spanish. Religion, politics, work, and recreation all have their Spanish vocabulary.

Don't panic. Take your time to learn new material, find somebody to answer your questions, look up words in the dictionary, and don't allow yourself to be intimidated by anything. Make mistakes and learn from them. When you goof up, you can either look mortified or just laugh about it—the choice is up to you.

Making the Most of the Spanish-Language Environment

Focus your attention on all things Spanish that you find in your daily life. Put yourself in situations where you have no choice but to use your Spanish. Begin to think in Spanish.

When you are in the thick of things, listen for key words. Try to identify the verb. Are there any pronouns you recognize? Does the word vaguely remind you of a word in English? Forget about trying to decode every single word—getting the main ideas first will help you fill in the details.

Listen for familiar intonation patterns and pay attention to the speaker's gestures. When you speak, don't be afraid to gesture as well. Nod your head and smile when you understand or agree. Twist your flat, horizontal palm back and forth for "so-so." Use your thumb and forefinger to indicate "a little bit."

To ask someone to clarify or repeat something, use the following phrases:

Perdón. ¿Cómo?
Excuse me. What?

¿Me lo repite más despacio, por favor?
Can you repeat it (what you said) for me more slowly, please?

Remember to relax and smile. Your audience is having as much trouble understanding you as you are having speaking. They want you to succeed. Take a deep breath and have a sense of humor about your mistakes. A smile goes a long way.

What You Already Know

In many places around the United States, Spanish is encountered at every turn—on street signs, on buses, at banks, and at restaurants. As soon as people begin learning Spanish, they discover that they know more Spanish than they had originally thought. In fact, Spanish is all over the world. Given the number of countries where Spanish is the official language, it most certainly ranks as one of the most widely spoken languages.

Recognizing Spanish-Sounding Words

To prove that you know more Spanish than you think you do, take a little quiz. Take a look at the following list, and see how many words you can understand.

accidente	cruel	motor
actor	doctor	musical
adorable	elefante	natural
animal	error	plan
asistir	famoso	popular
atractivo	favor	potente
auto	fútbol	presidente
autor	honorable	radio
catedral	hospital	respetable
central	hotel	simple
cereal	humor	taxi
ciclista	idea	teléfono
color	importante	usual
conductor	información	visible
convertible	inventor	
criminal	local	

Although you might not yet know how to pronounce these words in Spanish, you should be able to figure out what they mean, because all of these words are cognates. Cognates are words in different languages that share similar meaning and spelling because they originated from the same word. True cognates share the same meaning. Pure cognates are spelled identically in both languages. False cognates share a common origin and spelling but have completely different meanings.

Words such as *actor, animal, central, error, hospital, idea, natural, radio,* and *taxi* are pure cognates. (Note that even though these words are spelled the same way in English and in Spanish, the pronunciations are different.) Words like *accidente, autor, elefante, presidente,* and *teléfono* are true cognates—they share meaning but are only similar, not identical, in spelling.

But some cognates are false—although the pairs may look similar, they carry different meanings in different languages. Here's why: Many cognates between English and Spanish originated from Latin—hence the words "Latino" and "Latin America." Over time, these words gained new meanings in each language, and ended up evolving in completely different ways:

- *asistir:* "to attend" (not "to assist")
- *anciano:* "elderly" (not "ancient")
- *carta:* "letter," when referring to a form of written correspondence (not "cart" or "card")
- *chanza:* "joke" (not "chance")
- *constipado:* "congested," as when suffering from a cold (not "constipated")
- *delito:* "crime" (not "delight")
- *embarazada:* "pregnant" (not "embarrassed"—though misusing this word could certainly lead to embarrassment!)
- *fútbol:* "soccer" (not "football")
- *recordar:* "to remember" (not "to record")

Learning the Common Suffixes

From the true pure cognates, you may notice a one-to-one correspondence in Spanish and English of the following suffixes: *–al*, *–ble*, and *–or*.

-al (pertaining or related to; an extension of; a place)		
criminal	pertaining to crime	crimen (crime)
hospital	place for hospice and treatment	hospedar (to receive the needy)
usual	an extension of use, usual	usar (to use)
-ble (having the ability or aptitude to or capacity of; this suffix transforms verbs into adjectives)		
adorable	adorable, capable of being adored	adorar (to adore)
convertible	convertible, capable of being converted	convertir (to convert)
-or (agents that are or do; abstractions)		
inventor	inventor, one who invents	inventar (to invent)
amor	love	amar (to love)

Suffixes often clue you in on the meanings of the words that use them. A complete list of examples would be rather lengthy. Here are a few:

▼ SPANISH COGNATES WITH SUFFIXES -BLE, -AL, AND -OR

-ble	-al	-or
aceptable	anual	auditor
admisible	beneficial	compositor
biodegradable	cordial	destructor
blasfemable	cultural	detector
calculable	educacional	editor
curable	esencial	inferior
digestible	fatal	inspector
durable	federal	instructor
evitable	fundamental	mentor
falseable	ilegal	pastor
incomparable	nacional	profesor
lamentable	neutral	protector
miserable	oficial	reflector
negociable	original	rumor
organizable	parcial	seductor
ostensible	racional	superior

–ble	–al	–or
presentable	tradicional	valor
preferible	universal	vigor

From the other cognates, you see various suffixes that are familiar but just a little off:

–aje (pertaining to, particularly broadened to a collection; similar to English "–age")		
bagaje	military baggage	
equipaje	baggage	equipo (equipment)
–ano/–ana (pertaining to origin, location; relating to beliefs and affiliations; similar to English "–an")		
americano, americana	American (male, female)	
anciano, anciana	elderly man, woman	
–ante/–ente (related to an event, the nature of, or an agent; similar to "–ant" and "–ing" in English)		
accidente	an unexpected event	accidentar (to produce an unexpected event)
importante	something of great importance	importar (to import, to cause to matter)
potente	of powerful nature	poder (to be able to, power)
presidente	one who presides	presidir (to preside over)
–ción/–sión (abstraction of an act or state of being; similar to the English "–tion" and "–sion")		
atención	attention	atender (to attend, to pay attention)
información	information	informar (to inform)
–ico/–ica (relating to; being similar to; similar to the English "–ic" and "–al")		
físico	physical, physicist	física (physics)
idéntico	identical	identidad (identity)
–ista (pertaining to one who does; similar to English "–ist")		
ciclista	one who rides a bicycle	bicicleta (bicycle)
periodista	reporter, one who writes for a newspaper	periódico (newspaper)

−*ivo*/−*iva* (relating to an action; expresses tendency, disposition, or function; similar to English "−ive")		
atractivo	attractive	*atraer* (to attract)
extensivo	extensive	*extender* (to extend)
−*oso*/−*osa* (relating to possession or characteristic; similar to English "−ous," "−ful," and "−y")		
asqueroso	disgusting	*asco* (disgust)
famoso	famous	*fama* (fame)
−*ura* (abstraction of an act or state of being; similar to English "−ture," "−ure," and "−ness")		
criatura	baby, small child	*criar* (to breed and rear)
cultura	culture	*culto* (cultured)

Other suffixes to remember include those in the following tables:

−*ario*/−*aria* (pertaining to the subject; relating to an act or thing; similar to English "−ary")		
millonario	millionaire	*millón* (million)
voluntario	voluntary	*voluntad* (free will)
−*ncia* (relating to an act or state; result of an action; abstraction; similar to English "−nce" and "−ncy")		
abstinencia	abstinence	*abstener* (to abstain)
elegancia	elegance	*elegante* (elegant)
insistencia	insistence	*insistir* (to insist)
−*dad* (relating to an abstraction and a state of being; similar to English "−ty," "−ness," and "−hood")		
brevedad	brevity	*breve* (brief)
claridad	clarity	*claro* (clear, light)
enfermedad	sickness, disease	*enfermo* (sick)
−*ismo* (pertaining to an action or practice; state or condition; principles similar to "−ism")		
atletismo	athleticism	*atleta* (athlete)
idealismo	idealism	*idea* (idea)
−*mente* (pertaining to the manner, the timing, and the place of an action; similar to "−ly")		
afortunadamente	fortunately	*fortuna* (fortune)
relativamente	relatively	*relacionar* (to relate)

You already know so much Spanish! Take a look at all the words you know again. Look up the words you're not sure of. There will be times when you find words that are so obviously close to the English that you wonder why you didn't figure it out on your own. Take heart. When that happens, you probably will never have to look up that word again.

CHAPTER 2

Pronunciation

Now that you're convinced that you already know a lot of Spanish words, the issue comes down to injecting that certain Spanish flavor, that secret *salsa*, into them. In the following sections you will learn the Spanish alphabet and then take a look at the Spanish vowels and consonants.

Learning the Alphabet

In Spanish, the alphabet is called *el abecedario* (ehl ah-beh-seh-DAH-ryoh). When you take a look at the alphabet, you will see how similar it is to the one we use in English. For the most part, the Spanish letters are the same graphically as those employed in English. What's nice about them is that, unlike their American-English counterparts, their pronunciation is consistent (most of the time!), which makes learning to read in Spanish a whole lot easier.

▼ *EL ABECEDARIO* (THE SPANISH ALPHABET)

Letter	Spanish Pronunciation	Letter	Spanish Pronunciation
a	ah	n	EH-neh
b	beh	ñ	EH-nyeh
c	seh	o	oh
ch	cheh	p	peh
d	deh	q	koo
e	eh	r	EH-reh

Letter	Spanish Pronunciation	Letter	Spanish Pronunciation
f	EH-feh	s	EH-seh
g	hheh	t	teh
h	AH-cheh	u	oo
i	ee	v	veh
j	HHOH-tah	w	DOH-bleh veh
k	kah	x	EH-kees
l	EH-leh	y	ee GRYEH-gah
ll	EHL-yeh, EH-yeh	z	SEH-tah, ZEH-tah
m	EH-meh		

 Fact

There used to be another letter in the Spanish alphabet, *rr*, but it was officially dropped by the Royal Academy of Spain in the nineties. It was rumored that other double letters, *ch* and *ll*, would be dropped as well, but such hasn't been the case.

▼ **QUICK PRONUNCIATION GUIDE**

Letter	Pronunciation	Example	English
a	"a" in "father"	*mano* (MAH-noh)	hand
b	"b" in "box"	*bella* (BEH-yah)	pretty
c	"c" in "call"	*caja* (KAH-hhah)	box
	"c" in "city"	*cine* (SIH-neh)	movies
ch	"ch" in "change"	*chicle* (CHIH-kleh)	gum
d	"d" in "deck"	*día* (DIH-ah)	day
e	"e" in "pen"	*pera* (PEH-rah)	pear
f	"f" in "fine"	*fe* (feh)	faith
g	"g" in "go"	*ganar* (gah-NAHR)	to win
	a hard "h"	*gemelo* (hheh-MEH-loh)	twin
h	silent	*hola* (OH-lah)	hello
i	"ee" in "seen"	*listo* (LIH-stoh)	ready
j	a hard "h"	*justo* (HHOOS-toh)	just

Letter	Pronunciation	Example	English
k	"k" in "karma"	*kiosco* (KYOH-skoh)	kiosk
l	"l" in "lick"	*lado* (LAH-doh)	side
ll	"y" in "yay" or "j" in "déjà vu"	*llanto* (YAHN-toh, ZHAHN-toh)	crying
m	"m" in "more"	*mayo* (MAH-yoh)	May
n	"n" in "nickel"	*nada* (NAH-dah)	nothing
ñ	similar to "ni" in "onion"	*niño* (NIH-nyoh)	child
o	"o" in "more"	*mosca* (MOHS-kah)	fly
p	"p" in "open"	*país* (pah-EES)	country
q	"q" in "quiet"	*queso* (KEH-soh)	cheese
r	a hard "r" sound, like "tt" in "matter"	*oro* (OH-roh), gold	
s	"s" in "smart"	*sonar* (soh-NAHR)	to ring
t	"t" in "stay"	*tocar* (toh-KAHR)	to touch
u	"oo" in "boot"	*tuyo* (TOOH-yoh)	yours
v	between "v" and "b"	*vencer* (vehn-SEHR, behn-SEHR)	to overcome
w	"w" in "way"	*waterpolo* (wah-tehr-POH-loh)	water polo
x	"x" in "taxes"	*exilio* (eh-KSIH-lyoh)	exile
y	"y" in "yellow" or "j" in "déjà vu"	*yo* (yoh, zhoh)	I
z	"s" in "smart" or "z" in zebra	*zapato* (sah-PAH-toh, zah-PAH-toh)	shoe

Introducing the Vowels

Vowels, or *vocales* (voh-CAH-lehs), are letters representing sounds that are generated in the vocal cords without any obstruction from the mouth or lips, and can, on their own, form a syllable, or *sílaba* (SEE-lah-bah). Spanish vowels, when not accompanied by another vowel, have only one characteristic pronunciation, whereas their English counterparts have in excess of three. If you've mastered the fifteen-plus vowel sounds in English, you'll have no trouble with the five vowel sounds in Spanish.

The biggest difference between the five vowels in Spanish is that *a*, *e*, and *o* are considered "strong" vowels, while *i* and *u* are considered "weak" vowels. Notice also that the vowel *a* is pronounced by opening the mouth more than any other vowel. At the same time, both *o* and *e* are also pronounced with slightly less of an opening than *a*, while the more closed vowels *i* and *u* are articulated with only a slight opening. That is why some grammarians will label *a*, *e*, and *o* as "open vowels" while *i* and *u* are labled as "closed vowels."

 ## Question

What is a diphthong?
A diphthong is a combination of two vowels or vocalic elements that essentially become one combined sound, because both are pronounced within the same syllable.

The Vowel A

The first letter of *el abecedario* is the most open vowel of all vowels. That is why in Spanish it is sometimes called the "open vowel" or a *vocal abierta*. When saying it, your mouth is widely open and the distance between the palate and the tongue is at its greatest. You use the sound of *a* every day: What do you say when you go to the doctor and he asks you to open your mouth as he peers inside? Exactly! You say "ahhhhhhh." Now just skip the six extra h's and you have the Spanish letter *a*.

▼ **VOWEL *A***

Spanish	Pronunciation	English
ajo	AH-hho	garlic
altar	ahl-TAHR	altar
América	ah-MEH-rih-kah	America
árbol	AHH-bohl	tree
clavo	KLAH-voh	nail
fruta	FROO-tah	fruit

The strong vowel *a* combines with weak vowels (*i, u*) to make diphthongs (as in *aire* "air"). At the same time, other strong vowels (*o, e*) can also combine with the weak vowels (as in *hueso* "bone"). It is possible to see strong vowels consecutively in a word (*aéreo* "aerial, related to air"), but these vowels are not in the same syllable: *a-é-re-o*. When *a* is immediately in front of an unaccented *i* or *u*, the sound that is produced is neither a pure *a*, the dominant vowel in this case, nor a pure *i or u*, the weak vowels within the combination. As a result, the *ai* sound is not "ah-ee" but rather "i" as in "tie." The *au* resembles the "ahw" combination in "ouch."

What happens if the unaccented *i* or *u* precedes the *a*?

Diphthongs *AI* and *AU*

Spanish	Pronunciation	English
aire	AHye-reh	air
audaz	AHOO-dahs	bold
ausente	AHOO-sehn-teh	absent
auto	AHOO-toh	automobile
baile	BAHye-leh	dance

You've just seen how the *i* and the *u* submit to the stronger *a*, but what happens if another strong vowel challenges *a*? Well nothing, really. Each vowel keeps its own sound and is pronounced, as in the example *aéreo* "aerial."

▼ VOWEL COMBINATIONS *AE* AND *AO*

Spanish	Pronunciation	English
aéreo	ah-EH-re-oh	aerial
atraer	ah-trah-EHR	to attract
caer	kah-EHR	to fall
caos	KAH-ohs	chaos
maestro	mah-EHS-troh	teacher
paella	pah-EH-yah	Spanish rice dish

The Vowel *E*

E is the fifth letter of the alphabet, and is also a strong vowel. Pronounce it between the palate and the tongue by opening your mouth halfway. The letter *e* alone has the sound "eh," as in "get," and does not sound at all like the "ay" in "say," or "e" in "hyphen," "gene," "been," or "terse."

▼ VOWEL *E*

Spanish	Pronunciation	English
crecer	kreh-SEHR	to grow
estar	ehs-TAHR	to be (located)
hacer	ah-SEHR	to do, to make
joven	HHO-behn	young
nacer	nah-SEHR	to be born
necesito	neh-seh-SEE-toh	I need

As a *vocal fuerte* (strong vowel), *e* keeps its own sound when combining with other *vocales fuertes*.

▼ COMBINATIONS *EA*, *EE*, AND *EO*

Spanish	Pronunciation	English
crear	kreh-AHR	to create
creer	kreh-EHR	to believe
deseo	deh-SEH-oh	desire, wish
peaje	peh-AH-heh	toll
peor	peh-OHR	worse
reaccionar	reh-ahk-see-oh-NAHR	to react
reanudar	reh-ah-noo-DAHR	to renew

▼ WORDS THAT BEGIN WITH *ES–*

Spanish	Pronunciation	English
esbelto	ehs-BEHL-toh	slender
esbozo	ehs-BOH-soh	first draft, outline
escala	ehs-KAH-lah	scale

Spanish	Pronunciation	English
escultura	ehs-hhool-TOO-rah	sculpture
especial	ehs-peh-see-AHL	special
estilo	ehs-TEE-loh	style
reanudar	reh-ah-noo-DAHR	to renew

Remember, a strong vowel forms diphthongs only with weak vowels. When *e* is immediately followed by an unaccented *i* or *u*, the sound produced is a blend—the *ei* sound becomes "ey" as in "haystack"; the *eu* generally resembles "ehw" (unless the *u* is accented or naturally stressed within the word).

▼ **DIPHTHONGS *EU* AND *EI***

Spanish	Pronunciation	English
afeitar	ah-fehye-TAHR	to shave
euforia	eh-oo-foh-REE-ah	euphoria
europeo	eh-oo-roh-PEH-oo	European
neumático	neh-oo-MAH-tee-koh	tire
reino	REHye-noh	kingdom
treinta	TREHyen-tah	thirty

When the positions are reversed, that is, when an unaccented *i* or *u* is immediately followed by an *e*, the sounds that are produced are both expected and surprising. As with the letter *a*, the *i* takes on a sound similar to "y" within the *ie* combination, like in the English word "yet." The *ue* combination is a little trickier to get right away because it can have two possible, mutually exclusive pronunciations. In many words, *ue* will have the "weh" sound, as in the English word "wet."

▼ **COMBINATIONS *IE* AND *UE***

Spanish	Pronunciation	English
cuento	KOOehn-toh	story
duelo	DOOeh-loh	sorrow
mientras	MEEehn-trahs	while
muebles	MOOeh-blehs	furniture

Spanish	Pronunciation	English
pueblo	POOeh-bloh	town, village
riesgo	REEehs-goh	risk
sediento	seh-DEEehn-too	thirsty
siempre	SEEehn-preh	always

In some cases, the *u* in the *ue* combination is *muda* (mute), and the diphthong is pronounced as *e*. The *u* becomes silent when *ue* is preceded by a *g* or a *q*.

▼ **VOWELS *UE* PRECEDED BY *G* OR *Q***

Spanish	Pronunciation	English
descargue	dehs-KAHR-geh	an unloading
guedeja	geh-DEH-hah	lion's mane
guerra	GEH-rrah	war
pagué	pah-GEH	I paid
parque	PAHR-keh	park
quemar	keh-MAHR	to burn
queso	KEH-soh	cheese
relampagueo	reh-lahn-pah-GEH-oh	lightning flash

The Vowel *I*

The *i* is spoken through the smallest opening between the palate and the tongue. When unaccompanied by other vowels, *i* most resembles the "ee" sound in the word "machine." It is never pronounced as the English letter "i" in "mint," "edible," or "site."

▼ **VOWEL *I***

Spanish	Pronunciation	English
avenida	ah-veh-NEE-dah	avenue
bistec	bees-TEHK	(beef) steak
cita	SEE-tah	appointment
fácil	FAH-seel	easy
gentil	henh-TEEL	courteous
marido	mah-REE-doh	husband

Remember that when followed by other vowels, the *i* is usually a weak part of the diphthong and is not sounded out.

▼ *IA*, *IE*, *IO*, AND *IU*

Spanish	Pronunciation	English
acariciar	ah-kah-ree-seeYAHR	to caress, to pet
ciego	seeEH-goh	blind
cielo	seeEH-loh	sky
hierro	YEEeh-rroh	iron (metal)
idioma	ee-deeYO-mah	language
pie	peeYEH	foot
piedad	peeyeh-DATH	pity, mercy
viuda	veeYOO-dah	widow

However, if the *i* is accented (*í*), it is pronounced as "ee" even though it may precede or follow another vowel.

▼ *í* WITH ANOTHER VOWEL

Spanish	Pronunciation	English
caída	kah-EE-dah	fall
día	DEE-ah	day
freír	freh-EEHR	to fry
frío	FREE-oh	cold
lío	LEE-oh	mess
maíz	mah-EES	corn
oír	oh-EEHR	to hear
país	pah-EES	country
panadería	pah-nah-deh-REE-yah	bakery
reír	reh-EEHR	to laugh

In *ui* combinations, as in the *ue* combinations, the *u* is silent when it is preceded by a *g* or a *q*. That is, the *ui* combination sounds like *i*.

Spanish	Pronunciation	English
Arequipa	ah-reh-KEE-pah	a city in Peru
guisado	ghee-SAH-doh	stew
guitarra	ghee-TAH-rrah	guitar
quiero	KEEyeh-roh	I want
quitar	kee-TAHR	to remove, to take away
siguiente	see-gheeYEHN-teh	following
siquiera	see-keeYEH-rah	at least

The Vowel *O*

The last of the strong vowels is *o*, a vowel spoken through a medium-sized opening between the palate and the tongue. *O* has the sound "oh," similar to but actually shorter than the "o" in the English word "toll."

▼ VOWEL *O*

Spanish	Pronunciation	English
golpe	GOHL-peh	blow, hit
mortal	mohr-TAHL	fatal
mozo	MOH-soh	waiter
olor	oh-LOHR	smell
olvidar	ohl-vee-DAHR	to forget
operar	oh-peh-RAHR	to operate
ojo	OH-hoh	eye
oro	OH-rroh	gold

⊖ Alert

In English, the letter "o" may be pronounced in four different ways: as in "cod," "bone," "lemon," or "now." In Spanish, however, it retains the same pronunciation—as long as it is not joined with another vowel.

Combinations with *o* follow the same rules as other strong vowels or originally weak vowels with an accent, with the one exception being the *ou* combination.

▼ **VOWEL *O* WITH OTHER VOWELS**

Spanish	Pronunciation	English
alcohol	ahl-KOH-OL	alcohol
cohibir	koh-ee-BEEHR	to inhibit
coincidir	kohyen-see-DEEHR	to coincide
oasis	oh-AH-sees	oasis
oigo	OHye-goh	I hear
poema	poh-EH-mah	poem
roedor	roh-eh-DOHR	rodent
toalla	toh-AH-lyah	towel
zoológico	soh-oh-LOH-hee-koh	zoo

The Vowel *U*

The last of the Spanish vowels is a normally weak vowel that is spoken through a small-to-medium opening between the palate and the tongue. The *u* often adopts the "oo" sound, as in "too."

▼ **VOWEL *U***

Spanish	Pronunciation	English
blusa	BLOO-sah	blouse
curso	KOOHR-soh	course
dulce	DOOL-seh	sweet
luna	LOO-nah	moon
menú	meh-NOO	menu
nube	NOO-beh	cloud
unir	oo-NEER	to unite
usar	oo-SAHR	to use
útil	OO-teel	useful

You've already seen many different *u* combinations. In general, an unaccented *u* in combination with other vowels takes on a sound similar to the English "w."

One exception to the rule is that *u* is mute in the following combinations: *gue, gui, que,* and *qui.* However, there are a few words where the *u* in the diphthong is NOT mute. To indicate that the *u* should be pronounced, a *diéresis* (¨) is added over it (*ü*).

▼ *CU, GU, GÜ, HU,* AND *QU*

Spanish	Pronunciation	English
antiguo	ahn-TEE-gwoh	old
averiguar	ah-veh-ree-GWAHR	to inquire
bilingüe	bee-LEEN-gweh	bilingual
cigüeña	see-GWEHN-nyah	stork
cuidar	kooyee-DAHR	to care for
desagüe	deh-SAH-gweh	drain
huevo	WEH-boh	egg
huir	oo-EER	to flee
máquina	MAH-kee-nah	machine
pingüino	peen-GWEE-noh	penguin
quedar	keh-DAHR	to stay
quien	KEEyehn	who

Similarly, if naturally stressed or accented within a word, *u* keeps its "oo" sound.

▼ ACCENTED VOWEL *U*

Spanish	Pronunciation	English
ataúd	ah-tah-EWD	coffin
baúl	bah-EWL	chest or trunk
grúa	GREW-ah	crane
laúd	LAH-EWD	lute

Congratulations! You've just finished the vowels. If you're feeling a little overwhelmed, don't worry. Just take a break and remind yourself that learning a language takes time. You'll begin to feel more comfortable as you continue.

Consonants

Spanish consonants are a little tougher than Spanish vowels—Spanish has a few more consonants than English, and when combined with other letters, some consonants take on different pronunciations.

The consonants are sounds that can only be pronounced with the help of vowels, and letters representing these sounds make up the rest of the Spanish alphabet. Most Spanish consonants are very similar to their English counterparts. The following sections will examine the Spanish consonants by breaking them down into smaller groups.

The Consonants *B* and *V*

B is a bilabial consonant, or consonant formed by putting your lips together. It is formed at the union of one's upper and lower lips and is a clipped version of the American English "b." (*M* and *p* also belong to the same category.) *V*, on the other hand, is a labiodental consonant in English, formed by the union of one's upper front teeth and lower lip. This sound is not present in Spanish, certainly not with the vibration that goes along with the English consonant. When that orthographic *v* shows up between vowels in Spanish, it has a "softer" sound that is still bilabial. It should be noted that Spanish does have another labiodental, the consonant *f*, which sounds just like the English "f."

▼ CONSONANTS *B* AND *V*

Spanish	Pronunciation	English
barón	bah-ROHN	baron
varón	bah-ROHN	male
baso	BAH-soh	I base
vaso	BAH-soh	glass
tubo	TOO-boh	tube
tuvo	TOO-boh	(s)he had

 **Essential**

It should be noted that if both letters *b* and *v* are found at the beginning of a word or following the nasals *m*, *n*, or *ñ*, the pronunciation is stronger, like the bilabial "b" in English. However, when these letters are located within a word, between vowels, the sound is much softer.

The Consonants C, K, and Q

C (except in the combinations *ce* and *ci*), *q*, and *k* share the American English "k" sound. For the two *c* exceptions, read on to the following section. The letter *ch* is also covered separately.

▼ **C, Q, AND K**

Spanish	Pronunciation	English
acabar	ah-kah-BAHR	to finish
aquel	AH-kehl	that (at a distance)
blanco	BLAHN-koh	white
coser	koh-SEHR	to sew, to stitch
kilo	KEE-loh	kilogram
mecánico	meh-KAHN-nee-koh	mechanic(al)
placa	PLAH-kah	license plate
sacar	sah-KAHR	to take out
quebrar	keh-BRAHR	to break
quedar	keh-DAHR	to remain
quijada	kee-HAH-dah	jaw

The Consonants C, S, and Z

The Spanish *s* is easy. It sounds the same as the American English "s." How you should pronounce *c* (in combinations *ce* and *ci*) and *z* will vary, depending on the dialect of Spanish you use. In Latin America and Andalusia (a region in southern Spain), they are also pronounced as "s." In most regions of Spain, *c* (when followed by *e* or *i*) and *z* sound like the American English "th" sound in "thin."

Fact

You might have noticed that natives of Latin America who learn English have difficulty with the "th" sounds in words like "thin" or "thought." That's because this sound does not occur in Latin American Spanish.

▼ *CE, CI, S,* AND *Z*

Spanish	Pronunciation	English
accidente	ahk-see-DEHN-teh	accident
acecinar	ah-seh-see-NAHR	to dry-cure
aceituna	ah-sehye-TOO-nah	olive
asesinar	ah-seh-see-NAHR	to murder
centeno	sehn-TEH-noh	rye
cerca	SEHR-kah	near
cintura	seen-TOO-rah	waist
ciruela	see-REWeh-LAH	plum
esbozo	ehs-BOH-soh	first draft, outline
lucir	loo-SEEHR	to shine
omisión	oh-mih-SEEohn	omission
posible	poh-SEE-bleh	possible
salpicar	sahl-pee-KAHR	to sprinkle
tasa	TAH-sah	rate
taza	TAH-sah	cup/bowl

The Combination *CH*

Ch (cheh) sounds like the American English "ch" in "church." Dictionaries published before 1994 listed *ch* as a separate letter after *c*. Now, words that begin with a *ch* can be found under the letter *c*, between *ce* and *ci*. Use the following table to practice words with *ch*.

Spanish	English
ancho	wide, broad
charla	conversation
chocolate	chocolate
chuleta	chop (cut of meat)
colchón	mattress
cuchillo	knife
echar	to throw out
poncho	poncho, cape

The Consonants *D* and *F*

The Spanish *d* is a dentolingual consonant. As such, it is pronounced a little more like "th" in the English words "the," "this," or "that," than like the "d" in "dad" (with clenched teeth) when it comes between vowels and in other contexts. Try to practice saying the Spanish *d* by placing the very tip of your tongue between your teeth and saying English words that begin with "d."

▼ CONSONANT *D*

Spanish	Pronunciation	English
debajo	deh-BAH-hoh	under(neath)
pedazo	peh-THAH-soh	piece
redondo	reh-THON-doh	round
suceder	soo-seh-THER	to happen
sudar	soo-THAHR	to sweat
tenedor	teh-neh-THOR	fork

Another labiodental consonant is the *f*, pronounced just like the English "f" in "food." In English, this same sound may be spelled out with the combination "ph," but in Spanish, the combination "ph" for an "f" sound does not exist, and only "f" is used. So the English word "telephone" is *teléfono* in Spanish.

▼ **CONSONANT F (JUST LIKE IN ENGLISH)**

Spanish	English
diferente	different
difícil	difficult
elefante	elephant
fácil	easy
febril	feverish
ferocidad	fierceness
fiar	to trust, to lend
fijar	to fasten

The Consonants G and J

When *g* is followed by any consonant or *a*, *o*, or *u*, it sounds like the American English "g" in "golf." In combinations *ge* and *gi*, it carries a sound not found in American English—an overemphasized "hh" that starts at the back of the throat.

▼ **CONSONANT G**

Spanish	Pronunciation	English
bolígrafo	boh-LEE-grah-foh	pen
gordo	GOHR-doh	fat
gozar	goh-SAHR	to enjoy
grueso	GROOeh-soh	thick, stout
guardar	gwahr-DAHR	to store
gusano	goo-SAHN-noh	worm, caterpillar
gusto	GOOS-toh	pleasure
rogar	rohr-GAHR	to plead
vergüenza	behr-GWEN-sah	shame, shyness

But . . .

Spanish	Pronunciation	English
escoger	ehs-koh-HHER	to choose
exigir	ehk-see-HHEER	to demand

Spanish	Pronunciation	English
genial	hhen-nee-AHL	pleasant
lógico	LOH-hhee-koh	logical

The letter *j* represents the same "hh" sound as the one you just heard in combinations *ge* and *gi*. Note that the sound of "j" in "Jack" does not occur in Spanish.

▼ CONSONANT *J*

Spanish	Pronunciation	English
ejemplo	eh-HHEN-ploh	example
ejército	eh-HHER-see-toh	army
joya	HHOY-yah	jewel
juez	HOOyehs	judge
masaje	mah-SAH-hheh	massage
paisaje	pahyee-SAH-hheh	landscape
reloj	reh-LOHH	watch

The Consonant *H*

H in Spanish is a relic—once upon a time, it was used to designate an aspirated sound that no longer exists. Today, it is silent, unless it is coupled with the letter *c* to denote "ch."

▼ CONSONANT *H*

Spanish	Pronunciation	English
desahogo	deh-sah-OH-goh	emotional relief
exhalar	ek-sah-LAHR	to exhale
hábil	AH-beel	skillful
hábito	AH-bee-toh	habit
hablar	ah-BLAHR	to speak
humilde	oo-MEEL-theh	humble
rehusar	reh-oo-SAHR	to refuse

The Consonants *L* and *LL*

The single *l* is among the few letters that consistently has the same exact pronunciation in Spanish as in English. The pronunciation of *ll*, however, varies depending on where the speaker is from.

 **Essential**

You might hear the *ll* combination pronounced like "y" in "yellow," the "ly" sound in "million," the "j" sound in "treasure," or the "sh" sound in "she." All are considered correct, though it will help if you stick with one pronunciation consistently.

▼ **THE CONSONANT *L* (SAME AS ENGLISH)**

Spanish	English
ladrón	thief
lechuga	lettuce
licencia	license
lodo	mud
lujo	luxury
perla	pearl
sal	salt

▼ **THE SOUND *LL***

Spanish	Pronunciation	English
caballo	kah-BAH-lyoh	horse
cabello	kah-BEH-lyoh	hair
hallar	ah-LYAHR	to find
millón	mee-LYOHN	million
zambullir	sahn-boo-LYEER	to dive

The Consonants M, N, and Ñ

M and *n* have the same sounds as their respective English counterparts, except for a curious difference: In similar words in English and Spanish, the English "mm" or "nn" is usually dropped in favor of a single "m" or "n," though occasionally the double "n" is kept.

▼ *M* AND *N* (SAME AS ENGLISH)

Spanish	English
anual	annual
anunciar	to announce
comercial	commercial
innovar	to innovate
inocente	innocent
interesante	interesting
mojado	wet
recomendar	to recommend

M and *n* are fairly easy to understand—they are very similar to their English counterparts. However, what about that *ñ*? The closest American English approximation to *ñ*, pronounced "EH-nyeh," is the "ni" sound in "onion."

▼ CONSONANT *Ñ*

Spanish	Pronunciation	English
acompañar	ah-kohn-pah-NYAHR	to accompany
año	AHN-nyoh	year
compañero	kohn-pah-NYEH-roh	companion
niñez	nee-NYEHS	childhood
puño	POON-nyoh	fist
reñir	reh-NYEEHR	to quarrel

The Consonant *P*

P is very similar to the American English "p," minus the trailing breath. The clipped nature of both *b* and *p* often leads to confusing one with the other. Note that the combination "pp" does not occur in Spanish, so the Spanish version of the verb "appear" is spelled *aparecer,* with one *p*.

▼ CONSONANT *P* (SIMILAR TO ENGLISH, BUT WITHOUT ASPIRATION, OR THE BREATH THAT FOLLOWS INITIAL SOUND)

Spanish	English
aplicar	to apply
episodio	episode
hipo	hiccup
oponer	to oppose
oprimir	to press, oppress
papel	paper, role
pelea	fight
platicar	to chat
poesía	poetry

The Consonant *R* and Combination *RR*

The Spanish *r* is the letter that gives people the most trouble, because it must be trilled. Remember that all *rr*s and the *r*s at the beginning of a word are generally held longer than the rest.

▼ CONSONANT *R*

Spanish	Pronunciation	English
bucear	boo-seh-AHR	to scuba dive
Corea	koh-RREH-ah	Korea
ferrocarril	feh-rroh-kah-RREEL	railroad
radiografía	RRAH-deeyo-grah-FEE-ah	X-ray picture
raíz	RRAH-ees	root, origin
reto	RREH-toh	challenge
sierra	SEEyah-RRAH	mountain range
terreno	the-RREH-noh	land, field

The Consonant *T*

The Spanish *t* sounds similar to the "t" in "total." *T,* however, is pronounced with a short burst and the tip of the tongue positioned between both sets of teeth. The difference in these sounds is very subtle. Keep in mind, also, that Spanish does not have the "th" or "tt" combinations.

▼ **CONSONANT *T* (SIMILAR TO ENGLISH, WITHOUT ASPIRATION, OR THE BREATH THAT FOLLOWS INITIAL SOUND)**

Spanish	English
atención	attention
atraer	to attract
autor	author
catedral	cathedral
tela	fabric
tinto	tinged, red (wine)
tomar	to take, to drink
tomate	tomato
triste	sad

The Consonants *X* and *Y*

The letter *x* has different pronunciations depending on its position within the word. Between vowels, within letter combinations *exce–* and *exci–*, and at the end of the word, it sounds like "ks" or "gs." In some regions, when an *x* begins a word or is situated in between a vowel and a consonant, it has an "s" sound. In some words, it sounds the same as the Spanish *ge* or *j* (that is, like an overemphasized American English "h"). It also takes on a "sh" sound in some words that originate from indigenous Latin American languages. But don't worry about trying to memorize all these rules. Fortunately, you won't encounter the Spanish *x* very often.

▼ **CONSONANT *X***

Spanish	Pronunciation	English
examen	ehk-SAH-mehn	exam
excelente	ehk-she-LEHN-teh	excellent

Spanish	Pronunciation	English
excitante	ehk-see-TAHN-teh	exciting
extranjero	ehks-trahn-HEH-roh	foreigner
mexicano	meh-hee-KAHN-noh	Mexican
texano	the-HAHN-noh	Texan
xilófono	hee-LOH-phoh-noh	xylophone

You might have learned a long time ago that the American English vowels included "a," "e," "i," "o," "u," and sometimes "y." Though not considered "a vowel" in the strictest sense, the Spanish *y* usually acts like the vowel "i" when it sounds like the "y" in "yam." *Ay, ey,* and *oy* share their pronunciations with *ai, ei,* and *oi,* respectively; *uy* sounds like "oo-y." On its own, *y* sounds like "ee."

▼ CONSONANT **Y**

Spanish	Pronunciation	English
apoyo	ah-POH-yoh	support
hay	AHee	there is, there are
hoy	OHee	today
muy	MOOyee	very
raya	RAH-yah	line
rey	REHyee	king
suyo	SOO-yoh	yours
yerno	YEHR-noh	son-in-law

You've done it! You've just completed the Spanish alphabet! Take this time to pat yourself on the back—you deserve it.

Introducing Accent Marks

Now that you know how to read each Spanish letter, you need to learn something else that will help you read words in Spanish—the rules for choosing which syllable in a word should be stressed, and the purpose of accent marks.

In Spanish, there is one accent mark (*el acento agudo*, an acute accent mark), denoted as (´) and placed over the vowel to indicate that the syllable should be stressed. Only the words that do not follow the rules of Spanish actually have accent marks. These rules are:

- If a word ends with *n*, *s*, or a vowel, the emphasis is generally placed on the second-to-last syllable within that word. These words are known as *palabras llanas*. For example, in the word *zapato* ("shoe"), the next-to-last syllable is stronger, so it's pronounced sah-PAH-toh.
- If a word ends in a consonant other than *n* or *s*, the emphasis is generally placed on the last syllable within that word. These words are known as *palabras agudas*. For example, the word *coronel* ("colonel") is pronounced koh-roh-NEHL, where the last syllable is stronger.

If a word is not stressed according to these simple rules, the accented (or stressed) syllable is denoted with an accent mark. Every Spanish word is classified in terms of where the word is accented, implicitly or explicitly. In addition to *llanas* and *agudas*, words are also categorized as *esdrújulas* (accented on the third-to-last syllable) and *sobresdrújulas* (accented on the fourth-to-last syllable and beyond). All *esdrújulas* carry an accent mark.

Accents provide you with more than a pronunciation guide. In English, some words require context to know their pronunciation and meaning. Compare "The **pro**ject is due tomorrow" and "He wanted to pro**ject** an air of confidence." In Spanish, accent marks are sometimes used to help distinguish words. Take a look at a few examples that follow. Note that the only difference between these pairs is the accent mark—their pronunciations are exactly the same.

▼ **EXAMPLES OF USING ACCENT MARKS TO DISTINGUISH WORDS**

Spanish	English
él	he
el	the (definite article used with male nouns)
qué	what
que	that
quién	who (question word)
quien	who
sólo	only
solo	alone

CHAPTER 3

Subjects

As you might remember from grade school, every sentence has at least one subject—the thing or person who performs the action indicated by the verb. The following sections will give you all you need to know about the subject of a Spanish sentence to get you on your way to start putting together complete sentences.

Determining the Gender

Most of the time, the subject of your sentence will be a noun. Nouns work the same way in Spanish as they do in English—with one major exception. In Spanish, all nouns have an assigned gender, whether the noun represents a person, place, or thing. The gender of a noun is either natural, referring to people who do have an established gender, or grammatical, where gender has been arbitrarily assigned to things or concepts.

Natural Gender

Most nouns in this category come in two versions: masculine and feminine. Take a look at the following table.

▼ NATURAL-GENDER NOUNS

Masculine	Feminine
doctor (male doctor)	*doctora* (female doctor)
estudiante (male student)	*estudiante* (female student)
hombre (man)	*mujer* (woman)

Masculine	Feminine
inglés (Englishman)	*inglesa* (Englishwoman)
muchacho (boy)	*muchacha* (girl)
periodista (male journalist)	*periodista* (female journalist)
perro (male dog)	*perra* (female dog)
toro (bull)	*vaca* (cow)

There are four basic rules for dealing with natural gender nouns:

- When a masculine noun ends in –*o*, substitute an –*a* to make it feminine. For example, *muchacho* becomes *muchacha*, and *perro* becomes *perra*.
- When a masculine noun ends in a consonant, add an –*a* at the end to make it feminine. For example, *doctor* becomes *doctora*, and *inglés* becomes *inglesa*.
- Sometimes nouns have only one gender. For example, there is no feminine noun for *hombre*, so use *mujer*; *toro* becomes *vaca*.
- Sometimes the same word may be used for both genders; in these cases, the gender is specified by articles or adjectives. This rule includes (but is not limited to) words that end in –*ista* or –*e*. For example, *el periodista* becomes *la periodista*, *el estudiante* becomes *la estudiante*, and *el modelo* becomes *la modelo*.

Grammatical (Assigned) Gender

Grammatical gender does not follow a logical pattern and must be memorized. You can, however, identify some cases of grammatical gender by looking at the endings.

▼ MASCULINE ENDINGS

Ending	Example	English	Feminine Exceptions
–*aje*	*viaje*	journey	n/a
–*gen*	*origen*	origin	*imagen* (image), *margen* (margin)
–*men*	*examen*	exam	n/a

Ending	Example	English	Feminine Exceptions
−o	*libro*	book	*mano* (hand)
−or	*doctor*	male doctor	*labor* (work)

▼ FEMININE ENDINGS

Ending	Example	English	Masculine Exceptions
−a	*libra*	pound, lb.	*mapa* (map); some abstract nouns, like *problema*
−ad	*verdad*	truth	n/a
−ed	*merced*	mercy	n/a
−ie	*serie*	series	n/a
−ión	*religión*	religion	some concrete nouns, like *gorrión* (sparrow)
−sis	*síntesis*	synthesis	*análisis* (analysis), *énfasis* (emphasis), *éxtasis* (ecstasy)
−ud	*salud*	health	*ataúd* (coffin)
−umbre	*costumbre*	custom	n/a

Some nouns are feminine even though they end with an −o because they are really abbreviations. For example, *foto* (photo) is a feminine noun because it is really *fotografía* (photograph), a noun that ends with an −a.

An "S" for Plural

Making nouns plural is easy, because in most cases the concept is the same as in English—just add an −s or an −es. However, there are some variations, so take a look at the following rules:

- When the noun ends with an unstressed vowel, just add an −s. For example, *playa* (beach) becomes *playas* in plural.
- When the noun ends with a consonant other than −s, add an −es. For example, *flor* (flower) becomes *flores* in plural.

- When the noun ends with a stressed vowel, add an *–es*. For example, *iraní* (Iranian) becomes *iraníes*; *inglés* (Englishman) becomes *ingle-ses* in plural.
- When the noun ends with an unstressed vowel and *–s*, don't add anything. For example, *crisis* remains *crisis* in the plural.

How Articles Can Help

So far, all these rules may have left you dismayed. Do you really have to keep all those noun endings in mind just to establish the gender? Well, here is where the articles can help. Once you know the article, you can figure out whether the noun is feminine or masculine, singular or plural. Just as in English, Spanish articles come in two categories: definite and indefinite.

Definite Articles

Think of the definite article as one pointing to a concrete noun. In English, we've only got one: "the." In Spanish, you have four forms, depending on the noun's gender and number (one or more than one).

▼ **DEFINITE ARTICLE ("THE")**

Number	Masculine	Feminine
Singular	*el*	*la*
Plural	*los*	*las*

With the exception of proper names, Spanish articles are employed liberally with most nouns, even in places where the translation into English would drop them. And please don't forget to keep conjugating (or matching) your articles and your nouns—they must always match in gender and number.

 **Essential**

> When you learn a new noun, use the following strategy: Rather than making up mnemonic devices or memorizing complicated rules, memorize nouns with *la* or *el* before the singular form—it's the easiest way to keep track of their grammatical gender. For example, just as long as you remember that "the house" is *la casa*, you will know that this noun is feminine.

Exceptions to the Rule

How a word is stressed plays a significant role in determining the article used with it, so the exception rule goes as follows: A masculine article is always used before the singular form of a word beginning with a stressed *a* or *ha*. Take a look at some examples in the following table.

▼ **FEMININE NOUNS THAT TAKE ON THE MASCULINE ARTICLE IN THE SINGULAR**

Singular	Plural	English
el agua	*las aguas*	the water(s)
el águila	*las águilas*	the eagle(s)
el alma	*las almas*	the soul(s)
el ave	*las aves*	the bird(s)

An Aside on Prepositions

Here is another important point to remember: When the definite article follows prepositions *a* or *de*, they form a contraction: *a* + *el* = *al*; *de* + *el* = *del*. Try pronouncing *a el* quickly and then switch to *al*; you'll quickly see why Spanish speakers formed this contraction: It's a lot easier and faster to pronounce. And the same goes for the transformation from *de el* to *del*. It is important to note that when you see *a* + *él* in a sentence, no contraction occurs. That is because the *él* (meaning "he," third person singular pronoun) is stressed, as can be seen by the orthographic accent, and remains a separate word.

A Matter of Meaning

Some nouns have both a masculine form and a feminine one—which means the meaning differs based on what article it travels with. For example, take the word *capital.* Your first guess should be that it's masculine, and it can be: *El capital* means "capital," as in money. But—surprise, surprise!—there's also a feminine *capital* with an entirely different meaning. *La capital* is a capital of a city or country. And the two terms are not interchangeable.

▼ NOUNS THAT RELY ON ARTICLES FOR MEANING

Masculine Noun	English	Feminine Noun	English
el cólera	the cholera	la cólera	the anger
el coma	the coma	la coma	the comma
el cometa	the comet	la cometa	the kite
el corte	the cut	la corte	the court
el cura	the priest	la cura	the cure
el frente	the front line (in battle)	la frente	the forehead
el guía	the person who guides	la guía	the book, booklet, or female guide
el orden	the order (opposite of chaos)	la orden	the order (command, request)
el pez	the fish	la pez	the tar
el policía	the police officer	la policía	the police force
el radio	the radius, the physical radio	la radio	the radio programming

Indefinite Articles

But don't forget, in addition to the four definite article forms, Spanish also boasts four matching indefinite articles. In English, there's really only one, "a," though it is modified to "an" before any word that begins with a vowel ("a book," but "an apple"), and it is only used with singular nouns (no such thing as "a books," right?). In Spanish, you have *un* or *una* (depending on the gender of the noun) as equivalents to "a" or "an," and the indefinite articles *unos* and *unas* when the nouns are plural—you might think of these articles as meaning "some."

 Alert

Note that in Spanish, *uno* means "one" (1) and *unos* and *unas* are the masculine and feminine versions of "some." When applying a Spanish "one" to a masculine noun, *uno* loses its final vowel. For example, *un libro* means "one book" or "a book," depending on context.

▼ **INDEFINITE ARTICLES ("A," "AN," OR "SOME")**

Number	Masculine	Feminine
Singular	*un*	*una*
Plural	*unos*	*unas*

For example:

Hay unos carros en el estacionamiento.
There are some cars in the parking lot.

Hablé con unas chicas bonitas.
I talked to some pretty girls.

Es una actitud amistosa.
It's a friendly attitude.

Allí hay un banco.
There is a bank over there.

From Nouns to Pronouns

A subject may be a noun or a pronoun; basically, pronouns are words that are used to substitute for nouns: "You" can replace "the reader," "his" may be used instead of "John Smith's," and "them" might refer to "the students." In English, "I," "we," "you," "he," "she," "it," and "they" are known as subject pronouns. In Spanish, there are just a few more pronouns to choose from, because there are multiple versions for that humble word "you."

▼ PERSONAL PRONOUNS IN ENGLISH

Person	Singular	Plural
First person	I	we
Second person	you	you (or you all)
Third person	he, she, it	they

▼ PERSONAL PRONOUNS IN SPANISH

Person	Singular	Plural
First person	*yo*	*nosotros* (m), *nosotras* (f)
Second person (informal)	*tú*	*vosotros* (m), *vosotras* (f)
Third person	*él* (m), *ella* (f), *ello*	*ellos* (m), *ellas* (f)
Second person (formal)	*usted*	*ustedes*

Subject pronouns in Spanish and English are organized by person (first, second, or third) and number (singular or plural), but when you compare the two tables, you will notice a number of differences.

 Question

What is a grammatical person?
Basically, it's the point of view. First person is from the point of view of the speaker (I did this, we did that). Second person is from the point of view of the person being spoken to (you did that, why don't you . . . ?). Third person is from the point of view of another person, neither the speaker nor the listener (he did this, they did that).

The most obvious difference is the additional third person category. *Usted* and *ustedes* are second-person pronouns because they translate as "you" and deal with the person being spoken to. However, in Spanish they follow the same conjugation patterns as the third person. That's because *usted* is an old contraction of *vuestra merced* (your mercy), a very formal address that was made in third person (just as in English you would say "your mercy wishes," or less formally, "you wish").

In the plural, only use *nosotras, vosotras,* or *ellas* when all members of the group are female (or, in the case of *ellas,* all objects represented are feminine-gender nouns). When referring to males or mixed groups, use the masculine versions of the pronouns. For example, *las casas* (the houses) are *ellas,* but *los actores y las actrices* (the actors and actresses) are *ellos.*

"You" and "You" and "You"

Have you noticed that the Spanish pronoun chart lists five forms of "you"—*tú, usted, ustedes, vosotros,* and *vosotras?* That's a lot of options for just one English word. But let's take things one at a time.

First, consider the number: Are you addressing one person or more than one? If one, your options narrow down to *tú* or *usted.* If more than one, you'll be choosing from *ustedes, vosotros,* and *vosotras* (more on the special *vosotros* and *vosotras* forms later).

Next, you have to consider whether to address the person or persons formally or informally. *Tú* and *vosotros/vosotras* are informal forms. *Usted* and *ustedes* are the formal versions ("your mercy" is a pretty exalted way of addressing someone, after all).

In English, you never have to worry about whether you should address people with a formal or informal "you," so this will definitely take some getting used to. And it's not always clear which form to use. A good rule of thumb is this: *tú* and *vosotros/vosotras* should be used to address your friends, or by permission only. In all other cases, start out with *usted/ustedes,* until the person or people you're talking to invite you to switch to the informal version. The verb for using the *tú* form is *tutear. Me puede tutear* means, "You can use the *tú* form with me."

Usted, Ustedes (Formal Address)	Tú, Vosotros, Vosotras (Informal Address)
Demonstrates respect	Demonstrates acceptance
Used with elders (including your parents)	Used with friends and people your age, as well as with younger people and children
Used with persons of rank or nobility	Used with colleagues (informality pre-established)
Used with strangers	Used with friendly acquaintances
Used to maintain social distance	Used to reduce social distance

It's All about Good Manners

Unless you are attending an event where informality is actually encouraged, remember that any initial meeting should begin with each party using the formal form of address, *usted*. An exception might be when you are being introduced to a friend's social circle. Try to pick up on social cues as offered by the people you are meeting. If the situation is social and the party you meet treats you informally, try to determine why they are being familiar. Is it because that person wants you to feel relaxed and as if you are within an accepting environment (a case to respond with *tú*)? Or is it that the person is much older than you are and has the social option of being familiar (a case where it's best to stick to *usted*)?

If the situation warrants it and you want to break the ice, encourage the person you meet to treat you informally—if this person requests that you do likewise, go ahead. If the person does not reciprocate this request, ask if you may address the person informally, and be prepared for any answer. There is nothing wrong with requesting familiarity as long as you do it formally and don't respond negatively to either answer. Here are some examples of what you might say:

¿Me permite tratarlo/tratarla a usted de tú?
Do you permit me to treat you inthe familiar?

¿Me permite tutearlo/tutearla?
May I use the familiar form of address with you?

¿Lo/La puedo tutear?
Can I use the familiar form of address with you?

Common Courtesy

Respect or courtesy (*la cortesía*) may be expressed in a variety of ways. In addition to the formality within verbs, you will find courteous titles similar to the ones used *en inglés* (in English).

▼ FORMAL TITLE

Formal Title		Abbreviation (Spanish)	Abbreviation (English)
señor García	Mr. Garcia	*Sr.*	Mr.
señora Robles	Mrs. Robles	*Sra.*	Mrs.
señorita Sánchez	Miss Sanchez	*Srta.*	Miss

As in English, Spanish uses *abreviaturas de cortesía*—notice that these abbreviations are capitalized, whereas the full words are capitalized only at the beginning of a sentence.

When addressing a person directly, it is customary to simply say the appropriate title followed by the person's last name:

¿Cómo está (usted), señor Smith?
How are you, Mr. Smith?

Buenos días, señorita Salgado.
Good morning, Miss Salgado.

However, when speaking about someone or when identifying yourself and others by title, the definite article is used appropriate to the person's gender:

La Sra. Menéndez vive en Lima.
Mrs. Menendez lives in Lima.

Yo soy el Sr. Gómez.
I am Mr. Gomez.

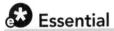 **Essential**

There are two other forms of address that you may come across: *don* and *doña*. Though once used as a title for nobility and land owner-ship, in many regions *don* and *doña* have simply replaced *señor* and *señora*. In some regions, the term *doña* has evolved into a criticism of sorts, equivalent to a "gossip" or a "busybody."

Politeness in Conversation

When you start a polite conversation, you can rely on one of the following greetings, depending on the time of day. You'll find these quite versatile—they may be used in both formal and informal situations.

buenos días	good morning (before noon)
buenas tardes	good afternoon (between noon and dusk)
buenas noches	good night (after dusk)

By its very nature, polite speech is very structured and almost formu-laic. In addition to a universal greeting, a typical encounter will likely include the following query and response:

¿Cómo está (usted)?
How are you?

Bien, gracias. ¿Y usted?
(I am) well, thank you. And yourself?

The following is a simple dialogue to help you practice what you have learned so far. The conversation is taking place at a conference; Linda Rodríguez and Alonso Calderón have never met before.

Linda: *Buenos días, señor.*
Good morning, sir.

Alonso: *Buenos días. Yo soy el Sr. Calderón, Alfonso Calderón.*
Good morning. I am Mr. Calderon—Alfonso Calderon.

Linda: *Linda Rodríguez, con mucho gusto. ¿Me permite tutearlo?*
Linda Rodriguez, nice to meet you. May I address you informally?

Alonso: *Sí. ¿Y yo la puedo tutear también?*
Yes, and may I address you informally too?

Linda: *Sí. ¿Cómo estás?*
Yes. How are you?

Alonso: *Muy bien, gracias. ¿Y tú?*
Very well, thanks. And you?

Linda: *Muy bien.*
Very well.

In Conjunction

You can string nouns together with conjunctions—those little words "and," "or," and "but." In Spanish, as in English, conjunctions are the connectors of words, phrases, and complete sentences. They may be divided into two broad forms:

- Those words that relate two or more items of equal function
- Those words that mark a dependence of one item on another

The two most basic conjunctions to learn are *y*, which usually translates as "and," and *o*, usually translated as "or" in English. As one-vowel words, these two conjunctions are vulnerable to a particular spelling change that is done to avoid two vowels colliding and losing the sound of *y* and *o*. When *y* precedes a word that begins with *i* or *hi*, it changes to *e*. For example, compare the following two sentences:

Yo soy inteligente y honesto.
I am intelligent and honest.

Yo soy honesto e inteligente.
I am honest and intelligent.

See, to avoid the "*y inteligente*" collision (if you were to pronounce this phrase correctly, you would have to drop one of the "ee" sounds because the *y* and the *i* sound exactly the same), the *y* transforms to *e*, which is pronounced "ey."

A similar spelling and pronunciation change occurs with *o*. When it precedes a word that begins with *o* or *ho*, this conjunction will change to *u*. For example:

Quiero seis o siete chocolates.
I want six or seven chocolates.

Quiero siete u ocho chocolates.
I want seven or eight chocolates.

Again, to avoid the collision of the two "oh" sounds in *o* and *ocho*, the conjunction *o* changes to *u* (pronounced "oo").

Other conjunctions in Spanish include *pero* (but), *ni . . . ni . . .* (neither . . . nor . . .), *que* (that), and *porque* (because).

CHAPTER 4

Verbs

In this chapter you will continue your development of self-expression by learning about the basic Spanish verbs. Your prior experience will provide you the conceptual tools for successfully completing this material. As with the previous sections, *relájate, y ¡adelante!* (relax, and forward!)—at your own pace, of course.

Working with Verbs

El verbo (the verb) is one of the most fundamental building blocks for Spanish expression. With it, you can often describe an action and who is performing that action. The simplest sentence *en inglés* (in English) requires a separate subject and predicate: "I am." *En español* (in Spanish), that sentence becomes simpler still: *Soy.* Because each verb is conjugated according to its subject, its ending will indicate who is doing the action—in this case, the pronoun *yo* (I) is optional and may be dropped.

A Spanish verb is made up of two parts: the base and the ending. Think of the base as the repository that holds the essence and definition of the verb, and the ending as the personal label indicating who owns the action and when it is occurring. For example: *Camino* (I walk) may be divided into *camin–* (the base) and *–o* (the ending that indicates a first-person singular subject "I" and that the verb is in the present tense of the indicative mood). Furthermore, verbs are subdivided into regular and irregular. To say a verb is regular is to say that its base is unchanged regardless of the ending employed and that its endings will follow regular patterns. An irregular verb's base might vary according to a specific conjugation, and some of its endings might be irregular as well.

 **Question**

What does "conjugate" mean?
To conjugate is to modify a verb based on such factors as number (singular or plural), person (first, second, or third), tense (past, present, future, etc.), or mood (indicative, command, or subjunctive). In Spanish, all verbs must be conjugated according to their subjects for number and person, and also according to the tense and mood that they convey.

The Verb's Mood

The grammatical "mood" isn't about how the verb is feeling—whether it's sad or gloomy or happy or confused. But in a way, it's not all that different. Any complete thought that you can convey possesses mood, also referred to as "voice," whether it is by what you say, how you say it, or under what circumstances you say it. When talking about the mood of an expression, you are focusing on the speaker's motivation in stating something in a particular way. The moods that you will encounter in Spanish fall under three general categories.

Indicative

Also known as the active voice, the indicative is the mood with which you express "what is" in an objective manner—by using facts, observations, and narration. You can argue (and many would probably agree) that no observation can be objective. This poses no problem in using the indicative; the use of this mood does not depend on truth so much as it depends on the speaker's motivation to lend authority to his or her statements. In a sense, you can say that it is the truth as she sees it and/or wishes to convince others to see it.

Imperative

With the imperative, you express actions as commands, warnings, and requests. Keep in mind that there are no imperious overtones with respect to a command. Also, *en español,* a command and a request are not opposites but actually equivalent. The same structure underlies both; the difference lies in the situation and the tone of voice that you employ.

Subjunctive

By using the subjunctive, you are expressing "what might be" or "what ought to be." This mood is contrary to the indicative in that it allows expression that is more apparently subjective. As such, it may express doubt, desire, emotion, impersonal opinion, or uncertainty. Native Spanish speakers employ the subjunctive naturally, so much so that it may become a holy grail of sorts for you to master after you become fairly proficient in the language.

The Most Basic Form: Infinitive

The infinitive allows you to speak of an action in the abstract, as a noun. In English, infinitives are verbs preceded by "to": to be, to go, to stay, and so on. Spanish infinitives do not have any function words equivalent to the English "to" that precede them, but you can recognize them by one of three possible endings: *–ar, –er,* and *–ir.* These three groupings aren't arbitrary—they signal how the verb should be conjugated. For every tense, you'll learn three sets of regular endings, one for each of these groups.

 **Essential**

Spanish verbs have tenses that correspond loosely with the English present tense, past tense, future tense, and so on. You will start with the present tense, and then go on to learn about other tenses as you make your way through the book.

The Present

Most language books teach present-tense verbs first, since these are generally the most straightforward and also the most useful. You can employ present-tense verbs in situations that describe the following:

- **An action that is occurring now.** For example: *Camino a la parada de bus.* (I walk/am walking to the bus stop.)
- **An ongoing experience.** For example: *Fumo demasiado.* (I smoke too much.)
- **A future act that will occur soon within a specified time frame.** For example: *Empiezo el trabajo dentro de un mes.* (I [will] start the job within a month.)
- **An act that you wish to convince yourself, or others, will occur.** For example: *Si encuentro un vestido rojo, lo compro.* (If I find a red dress, I [will] buy it.)

Conjugating Verbs in the Present Tense

First, let's take a look at conjugating regular verbs in the present tense. Remember: In order to conjugate a verb, you must first determine its infinitive form to figure out whether it belongs to the *–ar*, *–er*, or *–ir* category. Then, simply drop the infinitive ending and add the appropriate one to indicate correct person and number.

Look at the following table to see how to conjugate the regular verbs *cantar* (to sing), *aprender* (to learn), and *vivir* (to live). You may prefer to memorize the complete verb conjugations rather than just the endings—they'll help you remember how to conjugate other verbs in the present tense.

▼ *–AR* VERB ENDINGS

–ar	cantar	to sing (infinitive)
–o	(yo) canto	I sing
–as	(tú) cantas	you sing (informal, singular)
–a	(él, ella) canta	he, she, it sings
	(usted) canta	you sing (formal, singular)
–amos	(nosotros, nosotras) cantamos	we sing
–áis	(vosotros, vosotras) cantáis	you sing (informal, plural)
–an	(ellos, ellas) cantan	they sing
	(ustedes) cantan	you sing (formal, plural)

▼ −ER VERB ENDINGS

−er	aprender	to learn (infinitive)
−o	(yo) aprendo	I learn
−es	(tú) aprendes	you learn (informal, singular)
−e	(él, ella) aprende	he, she, it learns
	(usted) aprende	you learn (formal, singular)
−emos	(nosotros, nosotras) aprendemos	we learn
−éis	(vosotros, vosotras) aprendéis	you learn (informal, plural)
−en	(ellos, ellas) aprenden	they learn
	(ustedes) aprenden	you learn (formal, plural)

▼ −IR VERB ENDINGS

−ir	vivir	to live (infinitive)
−o	(yo) vivo	I live
−es	(tú) vives	you live (informal, singular)
−e	(él, ella) vive	he, she, it lives
	(usted) vive	you live (formal, singular)
−imos	(nosotros, nosotras) vivimos	we live
−ís	(vosotros, vosotras) vivís	you live (informal, plural)
−en	(ellos, ellas) viven	they live
	(ustedes) viven	you live (formal, plural)

 Question

Why do the *usted* and *ustedes* forms take on the verb forms of the third person?
Remember, the explanation is simple: *Usted* is an abbreviation of *vuestra merced* (your mercy), which technically corresponds to a third-person pronoun. In reality, *usted* (and *ustedes*) is a second-person pronoun that is used when addressing a speaker (or speakers) directly.

CHAPTER 5

Introducing *Ser*

The Spanish verbs *ser* and *estar* both translate as "to be," but they cannot be used interchangeably. In the following sections, you will learn how to distinguish between these two verbs, as well as the correct contexts for their usage.

Permanent States of Being: *Ser*

What if somebody were to ask you: "Who are you?" What would you say? How would you describe yourself?

¿Quién es usted?
Who are you?

Yo soy María Fernanda.
I am Maria Fernanda.

Soy profesora de matemáticas.
I am a math teacher.

Soy alta y rubia.
I am tall and blond.

Soy de Chile.
I am from Chile.

Maria's description of herself contains permanent facts: her name, her occupation, what she looks like, and where she is from. This is why she used *soy*, the *yo* form of the verb *ser*, to describe herself. *Ser* is an irregular verb, which means you can't just use the regular present-tense endings to conjugate it.

To learn how to conjugate *ser* in the present tense, take a look at the following table.

▼ **CONJUGATING *SER* IN THE PRESENT TENSE**

(yo) soy	I am
(tú) eres	you are (informal, singular)
(él, ella, usted) es	he, she, it is; you are (formal, singular)
(nosotros, nosotras) somos	we are
(vosotros, vosotras) sois	you are (informal, plural)
(ellos, ellas, ustedes) son	they are; you are (formal, plural)

Place of Origin

Use *ser* when discussing place of origin and nationality. For example:

¿De dónde es usted?
Where are you from?

Soy de Rusia.
I am from Russia.

¿Es usted ruso?
Are you Russian?

Sí, soy ruso. / Sí, lo soy.
Yes, I am Russian. / Yes, I am.

No, no lo soy.
No, I'm not.

Remember to add the right endings to words of nationality, depending upon whether they describe males or females, and whether they refer to one or many. For example, "American" may be *americano, americana, americanos,* or *americanas*. Unless there are irregularities, generally only the male singular form is provided.

▼ VOCABULARY: COUNTRIES AND THEIR CITIZENS

País (Country)	Ciudadano (Citizen)
Afganistán	*afgano,a*
Alemania (Germany)	*alemán, alemana*
Argentina	*argentino,a*
Australia	*australiano,a*
Austria	*austríaco,a*
Bélgica (Belgium)	*belga* (masculine and feminine)
Brasil	*brasileño,a*
Canadá	*canadiense* (masculine and feminine)
Chile	*chileno,a*
China	*chino,a*
Colombia	*colombiano,a*
Costa Rica	*costarricense* (masculine and feminine)
Ecuador	*ecuatoriano,a*
Egipto	*egipcio,a*
Francia	*francés, francesa*
Gran Bretaña (Great Britain)	*británico,a*
Grecia (Greece)	*griego,a*
Guatemala	*guatemalteco,a*
Haití	*haitiano,a*
Holanda	*holandés, holandesa*
India	*indio,a*
Inglaterra (England)	*inglés, inglesa*
Irán	*iraní* (masculine and feminine)
Iraq	*iraquí* (masculine and feminine)
Irlanda	*irlandés, irlandesa*
Israel	*israelí* (masculine and feminine)
Italia	*italiano,a*

País (Country)	Ciudadano (Citizen)
Jamaica	jamaicano,a
Japón	japonés, japonesa
México	mexicano,a
Nicaragua	nicaragüense (masculine and feminine)
Panamá	panameño,a
Perú	peruano,a
Polonia (Poland)	polaco,a
Puerto Rico	puertorriqueño,a
República Checa (Czech Republic)	checo,a
República de Eslovenia (Republic of Slovenia)	esloveno,a
El Salvador	salvadoreño,a
Sudáfrica (South Africa)	sudafricano,a
Suecia (Sweden)	sueco,a
Suiza (Switzerland)	suizo,a
Tailandia	tailandés, tailandesa
Turquía (Turkey)	turco,a
Venezuela	venezolano,a

 Alert

Notice that in Spanish you don't need to capitalize adjectives of nationality as you would in English, so "American" becomes *americano*, and so on. However, names of countries are capitalized in both languages.

Physical Characteristics

The adjectives in the following list describe characteristics that are permanent, meaning they don't change from day to day. They go with the verb *ser*.

▼ PHYSICAL-CHARACTERISTIC ADJECTIVES

alto	tall
anciano	elderly
bajo	short
bello	beautiful
bonito	pretty
calvo	bald
delgado	thin
elegante (masculine and feminine)	elegant
feo	ugly
fuerte (masculine and feminine)	strong
gordo	fat
grande	big, large
grueso	thick, stout
guapo	handsome
hermoso	beautiful
joven (masculine and feminine)	young
mayor (masculine and feminine)	older
moreno	dark-haired (can also refer to skin)
pelirrojo	redheaded
pobre (masculine and feminine)	poor
rubio	blond
viejo	old

Here are some examples of using a physical-characteristic adjective and the verb *ser:*

Los chicos son muy jóvenes.
The boys are very young.

Rosalinda es morena, con ojos oscuros.
Rosalinda is dark-haired, with dark eyes.

Vosotros sois unos tipos fuertes.
You are some strong guys.

Soy una chica muy guapa.
I'm a very pretty girl.

Ser and the Preposition *De*

You will often find yourself using the preposition *de* when describing personal characteristics with the verb *ser*. Though *en inglés* you would use two different prepositions, "of" and "from," *en español* you simply use *de*. *De* is often used to express a sense of belonging. In English, you have the construction "'s"—you can say "Charlie's book" or "kids' toys." In Spanish, that's not an option. Instead, you have to remember to flip the phrase around and use *de: el libro de Charlie* (the book of Charlie), *los juguetes de los niños* (the toys of the kids).

La mesa es de madera.
The table is made of wood.

Jonathan es de Chicago.
Jonathan is from Chicago.

La muñeca de Jenny es de Inglaterra.
Jenny's doll is from England.

Yo soy la hija de Luis y Ana Moncayo.
I am the daughter of Luis and Ana Moncayo.

El pan es de trigo.
The bread is made of wheat.

Yo estoy en clase de dos a tres.
I am in class from two to three.

Ella es de Chicago.
She is from Chicago.

Soy de estatura mediana.
I am of medium height.

Occupation

For the purposes of Spanish grammar, think of occupation as a reflection of one's identity, a permanent characteristic that goes with the verb *ser*. For example:

¿Cuál es su profesión? ¿Qué hace usted?
What is your profession? What do you do?

Soy actriz.
I am an actress.

As you can see, the indefinite article "a/an" isn't used before a person's profession. Now, here is some useful vocabulary to talk about professional occupations in Spanish.

▼ *LAS PROFESIONES* (OCCUPATIONS)

actor, actriz	actor, actress
amo,a (de casa)	homemaker
analista de inventario (masculine and feminine)	inventory analyst
arquitecto,a	architect
asistente ejecutivo,a	executive assistant
banquero,a	banker
camarero,a	waiter
consejero,a de inversiones	investment advisor
consultor(a) de mercadeo	marketing consultant
contador(a)	accountant
director(a)	director
diseñador(a)	designer
diseñador(a) de software	software developer
estudiante (masculine and feminine)	student

farmacéutico,a	pharmacist
gerente (masculine and feminine)	manager
ingeniero,a químico,a	chemical engineer
juez(a)	judge
maestro,a	teacher
médico,a	doctor
mercader(a)	merchant
modista (masculine and feminine)	dressmaker
músico,a	musician
pediatra (masculine and feminine)	pediatrician
periodista (masculine and feminine)	journalist
piloto (masculine and feminine)	pilot
profesor(a) de música	music teacher
repostero,a	pastry maker
sastre (masculine and feminine)	tailor
supervisor(a)	supervisor
tabernero,a	bartender
vendedor(a)	salesperson

Personal Relationships

The verb *ser* is used for describing personal relationships for the same reason that it is used to describe occupations—relationship roles are considered to be permanent characteristics. You will always be your parents' daughter or son, and they will always be your parents. While some relationships might not last quite as long, they are still considered permanent in the grammatical sense.

Carolina es la amiga de Estefi.
Carolina is Estefi's friend.

Las dos estudiantes son grandes enemigas.
The two students are great enemies.

Marco y Juan son socios.
Marco and Juan are associates.

Ellos son rivales.
They are rivals.

Elena es la hija de Sandra.
Elena is the daughter of Sandra.

Note that relationships that go with *ser* need not be family relationships.

Counting on *Ser*

Ser is also used in the language of numbers and counting. Think about it this way: The fact that two plus two is four is a permanent characteristic, not a temporary state, so you would say *dos más dos son cuatro*. Take a look at the following simple math equations and how to say them in Spanish.

$2 \times 2 = 4$
dos por dos son cuatro

$10 + 10 = 20$
diez más diez son veinte

$9 - 2 = 7$
nueve menos dos son siete

$8 \div 8 = 1$
ocho dividido por ocho es uno

The verb *ser* can also be used in discussing prices, where it can substitute for *costar* (to cost). For instance, compare the following two sentences:

El kilo(gramo) de manzanas es dos euros.
The kilogram of apples is two euros.

La copa de vino tinto cuesta siete dólares.
The glass of red wine costs seven dollars.

CHAPTER 6

Introducing *Estar*

Whereas *ser* is a verb of permanence, the verb *estar* (to be) is reserved for more transitory meanings. It will help you discuss such "temporary" points as the weather, your mood, and somebody or something's physical location—not just "temporary" elements, but in fact, states of "being."

Location and Temporary State

Estar can help you answer the questions "Where are you?" and "How are you?" Use this verb when referring to a person's physical location or temporary state of being. For example:

¿Cómo está usted?
How are you?

Estoy muy bien, gracias.
I'm very well, thanks.

¿Dónde está usted?
Where are you (located)?

Estoy en mi casa.
I'm at home.

The verb *estar* is conjugated in the present tense. *Estar* is another one of those irregular verbs, though it does not veer off the regular path quite as far as *ser*.

▼ **CONJUGATING *ESTAR* IN PRESENT TENSE**

(yo) estoy	I am
(tú) estás	you are (informal, singular)
(él, ella, usted) está	he, she, it is; you are (formal, singular)
(nosotros, nosotras) estamos	we are
(vosotros, vosotras) estáis	you are (informal, plural)
(ellos, ellas, ustedes) están	they are; you are (formal, plural)

Estar is often used when dealing within a time frame—the how, when, where, and who at a particular point in time. *¿Cómo está usted?* is a common social inquiry—part courtesy, part small talk, generally a way to catch up on current physical, mental/emotional, positional, and professional conditions.

Physical State

Match the verb *estar* with the adjectives and adverbs in the following table to describe how you feel. Keep in mind that adjectives and adverbs need to agree in person and number with their respective subjects. For example: *Él está cansado. Ella está cansada. Ellos están cansados. Ellas están cansadas.* (He/she/they are tired.)

▼ **VOCABULARY: DESCRIBING HOW YOU FEEL**

así así (masculine and feminine)	so-so
cansado	tired
débil (masculine and feminine)	weak
despierto	awake
dolorido	in pain
dormido	asleep
ebrio	drunk
enfermo	sick

mareado	dizzy
ocupado	busy
sobrio	sober

Usted no está mareado todavía.
You are still not dizzy.

Los niños están dormidos.
The kids are sleeping.

Yo estoy débil después de tanto trabajo.
I am (feeling) weak after so much work.

Mental State

In addition to physical conditions, *estar* is also used to describe mental and emotional conditions. The following table contains some vocabulary you will need to help you describe your state of being.

▼ **VOCABULARY: MENTAL AND EMOTIONAL CONDITIONS**

aburrido	bored
avergonzado	embarrassed
celoso	jealous
contento	satisfied, happy
enfadado	angry, annoyed
feliz (masculine and feminine)	happy
molesto	annoyed
preocupado	worried
temeroso	fearful

Yo estoy feliz.
I am happy.

Vosotros estáis tranquilos ya.
You are already (feeling) calm.

Estás loca con preocupación.
You are crazy with worry.

Point of Location

Estar also expresses a "positional" situation—where you are at a particular time, answering the question *¿Dónde está usted?* (Where are you?). Physical location may include an actual place (country, town, street, building, and so on), or a reference to a place in relation to a person's environment.

▼ *¿DÓNDE ESTÁ USTED? ESTOY:*

en México	in Mexico
en la calle Sucre	on Sucre Street
en casa	at home
aquí	here
acá	over here (in this general area)

Refer to the following table for a list of prepositions you can use to indicate the location of an object or person:

▼ **PREPOSITIONS**

a mano derecha	on the right
a la derecha de	to the right of
a mano izquierda	on the left
a la izquierda de	to the left of
al fondo de	at/in the back of
al lado de	to the side of, next to
abajo	down, downstairs
arriba	up, upstairs
adentro	inside
afuera	outside
cerca de	close to
lejos de	far from

debajo de	under
sobre	over, on top of
atrás	in the back
delante de	in front of
detrás de	behind
enfrente	in front (facing)

 Fact

In English, "where you are" isn't necessarily tied to a physical position but can also point to a position within a process. This also holds true for Spanish: *¿En qué día está en su dieta?* (On what day are you in your diet?) *Estoy en mi tercer día.* (I am on my third day.)

The following are some examples of sentences with prepositions you have just learned.

Los niños están afuera.
The children are outside.

La gasolinera está a mano derecha.
The gas station is on the right.

Celso está detrás de su amigo en la fila.
Celso is behind his friend in the line.

Yo vivo enfrente de una iglesia.
I live in front of a church.

Las llaves están sobre la mesa.
The keys are on top of the table.

César trabaja cerca de su casa.
Cesar works close to his home.

El regalo está debajo del árbol.
The present is beneath the tree.

Situational Prepositions

The "situational" aspect of *estar* is brought out by the prepositions that frequently follow it immediately. It is this aspect that makes it so flexible and as a result more widely used than *ser.*

Preposition *Con*

The preposition *con* (with) may be used to express physical proximity:

Estoy con mis padres.
I am with my parents.

It may also be used to express religious or ideological proximity:

Está con Dios.
He is with God.

Está con los demócratas.
She is with the Democrats.

Con is also used to express physical, mental, or emotional experiences (primarily used with nouns that describe a physical state):

Estoy con vergüenza.
I am embarrassed.

Preposition *Contra*

The preposition *contra* (against), sometimes used together with *en,* may be used to express physical contact or opposition to ideology or circumstances:

Estoy contra la pared.
I am against the wall.

Están en contra de la guerra.
They are against the war.

Estamos en contra del socialismo.
We are in opposition to socialism.

Preposition *De*

The preposition *de* (of, from) may be used to express physical position, mental position, a change in position, or a momentary condition. Here are some examples with the phrase *estar de:*

Estamos de pie.
We are standing (literally: on our feet).

Están de vacaciones.
They are on vacation.

Estamos de acuerdo.
We are in agreement.

Preposition *Entre*

The preposition *entre* (between) may be used to express physical position or mental or emotional condition (usually idiomatic). For example:

Estás entre amigos.
You are among friends.

Están entre la espada y la pared.
They are trapped. (Literally: They are between a sword and a wall.)

Estoy entre sí y no.
I am undecided (literally: between yes and no).

Preposition *Para*

The preposition *para* in combination with *estar* may be used to express a prepared condition, mood, or inclination to act for someone or something. Take a look at the following examples:

Estoy para llegar a casa.
I am about to arrive at home.

Estamos para ir a la tienda.
We are about to go to the store.

Está para fiestas.
He is generally open to parties.

Preposition *Por*

The preposition *por* (for), in combination with *estar,* may be used to express a reasoned or emotional preference for a person and ideology, or as a reasoned preference or contemplation of an act.

Estamos por los derechos humanos.
We are for human rights.

Estoy por ir al cine.
I am in favor of going to the movies.

Están por ir a la tienda.
They are going to go to the store.

Preposition *Sin*

The preposition *sin* (without) may be used to express a lacking condition:

Estoy sin dinero.
I am without money.

Estamos sin dormir.
We are without sleep.

Estar and the Present-Progressive Tense

Often, when translating the present tense of verbs, you will find some reference to the action as it progresses. It's not unusual to see *yo camino* translated as "I am walking." While the Spanish present tense does capture an action in the moment, it is more like a simple snapshot than a video. The present progressive is the tense that allows you to "see" the action as it is occurring.

It actually combines two different parts of speech, *estar* (conjugated according to the subject) and the present participle of the verb that shows action in progress, to realize a description of an action in movement. Think of the present progressive as the equivalent of the English construction "is –ing." To see how *cantar* (to sing), *aprender* (to learn), and *vivir* (to live) are conjugated in the present progressive, refer to the following table.

▼ **PRESENT-PROGRESSIVE TENSE**

yo estoy cantando, aprendiendo, viviendo
I am singing, learning, living

tú estás cantando, aprendiendo, viviendo
you are singing, learning, living (informal, singular)

él, ella, usted está cantando, aprendiendo, viviendo
he, she, you are singing, learning, living (formal, singular)

nosotros, nosotras estamos cantando, aprendiendo, viviendo
we are singing, learning, living

vosotros, vosotras estais cantando, aprendiendo, viviendo	
you are singing, learning, living (informal, plural)	

ellos, ellas, ustedes están cantando, aprendiendo, viviendo
they, you are singing, learning, living (formal, plural)

Here are some examples of how to use the present-progressive tense:

Jonathan está corriendo en el parque.
Jonathan is running at the park.

¿Estás hablando por teléfono?
Are you talking on the phone?

Mis padres están viviendo ahora en Madrid.
My parents are living in Madrid now.

As you learn other verb tenses, you will also discover that the construction of *estar + verbo* that forms the present-progressive tense, which you have just learned, also exists in other tenses: *yo estaba cantando* (I used to be singing), *estuve aprendiendo* (I was learning), *he estado viviendo* (I have been living), *yo estaré celebrando* (I will be celebrating).

Which Is Which?

To a native English speaker, it might not always be obvious when to use *ser* and when to use *estar*—in English, we have only one "to be" verb. To help you make the distinction, memorize the following general rules:

- *Ser* corresponds to expressions of permanent characteristics.
- *Estar* corresponds to description of situation.

For instance, compare the following pairs:

Ella es de Florida./Ella está en Florida.
She's from Florida./She is in Florida.

Ellos son felices./Ellos están felices.

They are happy people./They are happy (now).

For a more detailed list of rules on how to choose between *ser* and *estar*, refer to the following table.

▼ **RULES FOR USING *SER* AND *ESTAR***

Use *Estar*	Use *Ser*
situación física (physical situation)	*profesión, oficio, y actividad* (profession, occupation, and activity)
estado físico (physical state)	*parentesco y relaciones* (familial and other relationships)
estado mental (mental state)	*personalidad* (personality)
apariencia temporal (temporary appearance)	*apariencia característica* (characteristic appearance)
resultados de una acción (results of an action)	*posesión* (possession)
progreso de una acción (progress of an action)	*acción, con ocurrir o tener lugar* (action, when something occurs or takes place)
materia y origen (essence and origin)	
tiempo, cantidad, precio, y número (time, quantity, price, and number)	
construcciones de impersonalidad (impersonal constructions)	

CHAPTER 7

Other Verb Tenses

So far, the discussion of verbs has been centered on the present. But at any given moment, you might be remembering the past or looking toward the future. Just as verbs are conjugated according to person and number, they are also conjugated according to their point in time—their tense.

Conjugating Regular Verbs

Conjugating most Spanish regular verbs that you come across will be as simple as "plug and play." If you know who is acting and when the action is occurring in relation to you, simply attach the appropriate ending to the verb base and, like magic, you've expressed a complete thought in Spanish.

As you practice memorizing the tenses and their endings, apply verbs immediately to yourself and your situation and then extend your situation to others. Repetition will help you focus in on, and eventually internalize, the base of a few model verbs. At some point, probably when you least expect it, you'll start "sensing" how the thousands of regular verbs relate to these models, and you will have begun to conquer Spanish.

Preterite Tense

The preterite tense refers to the simple past and often to a single occurrence within one instance or recurring more specific instances. It is important to understand that the action is rooted in the past and physically and psychologically cut off from the present; the past action has terminated and is in effect complete (in grammar, complete tenses are known as "perfect" ones). The action may be tied to the past in terms of any of the following:

- *A particular moment or date.* For example: *Nací el 12 de junio de 1966.* (I was born on June 12, 1966.)
- *Several isolated instances.* For example: *Llamé cinco veces.* (I called five times.)
- *Duration.* For example: *En aquel año, trabajé en el Cuerpo de Paz.* (In that year, I worked in the Peace Corps.)

Conjugating Verbs in the Preterite Tense

Regular verbs may fall into the *–ar, –er,* or *–ir* category. The following table will provide you with the endings you need to learn in order to conjugate verbs in the preterite tense. The regular verbs used as examples are *cantar* (to sing), *aprender* (to learn), and *vivir* (to live). Note that in the preterite, the *–er* and *–ir* verbs share identical endings.

▼ *–AR* VERB ENDINGS IN THE PRETERITE TENSE

–ar	cantar	to sing (infinitive)
–é	(yo) canté	I sang
–aste	(tú) cantaste	you sang (informal, singular)
–ó	(él, ella) cantó	he, she, it sang
	(usted) cantó	you sang (formal, singular)
–amos	(nosotros, nosotras) cantamos	we sang
–asteis	(vosotros, vosotras) cantasteis	you sang (informal, plural)
–aron	(ellos, ellas) cantaron	they sang
	(ustedes) cantaron	you sang (formal, plural)

▼ *–ER* VERB ENDINGS IN THE PRETERITE TENSE

–er	*aprender*	to learn (infinitive)
–í	*(yo) aprendí*	I learned
–iste	*(tú) aprendiste*	you learned (informal, singular)
–ó	*(él, ella) aprendió*	he, she, it learned
	(usted) aprendió	you learned (formal, singular)
–imos	*(nosotros, nosotras) aprendimos*	we learned
–isteis	*(vosotros, vosotras) aprendisteis*	you learned (informal, plural)
–eron	*(ellos, ellas) aprendieron*	they learned
	(ustedes) aprendieron	you learned (formal, plural)

▼ *–IR* VERB ENDINGS IN THE PRETERITE TENSE

–ir	*vivir*	to live (infinitive)
–í	*(yo) viví*	I lived
–iste	*(tú) viviste*	you lived (informal, singular)
–ó	*(él, ella) vivió*	he, she, it lived
	(usted) vivió	you lived (formal, singular)
–imos	*(nosotros, nosotras) vivimos*	we lived
–isteis	*(vosotros, vosotras) vivisteis*	you lived (informal, plural)
–eron	*(ellos, ellas) vivieron*	they lived
	(ustedes) vivieron	you lived (formal, plural)

Imperfect Tense

The companion to the preterite, the imperfect tense also refers to the simple past. Whereas the preterite is enclosed by time, the imperfect is not. An action can have occurred over a span of time with no clear beginning or ending point. There may or may not be a connection with the present; it may or may not still be happening. The action of the imperfect tense may be tied to the following:

- *An unspecified amount of time.* For example: *De niño, quería un caballo.* (As a boy, I wanted a horse.)

- *An indefinite number of occurrences, such as a habit or custom.* For example: *Cada vez que la veía, me sentía feliz.* (Each time I saw her, I felt happy.)

Conjugating Verbs in the Imperfect Tense

The following table includes the verb endings for verbs in the imperfect tense. Notice that the *yo* form and the *él, ella, usted* forms of these verbs is the same. To avoid confusion, simply add the relevant pronoun to identify the correct person. And as with the preterite-tense endings, imperfect *–er* and *–ir* verbs share the same set of endings.

▼ *–AR* VERB ENDINGS IN THE IMPERFECT TENSE

–ar	cantar	to sing (infinitive)
–aba	*(yo) cantaba*	I sang
–abas	*(tú) cantabas*	you sang (informal, singular)
–aba	*(él, ella) cantaba*	he, she, it sang
	(usted) cantaba	you sang (formal, singular)
–ábamos	*(nosotros, nosotras) cantábamos*	we sang
–abais	*(vosotros, vosotras) cantabais*	you sang (informal, plural)
–aban	*(ellos, ellas) cantaban*	they sang
	(ustedes) cantaban	you sang (formal, plural)

▼ *–ER* VERB ENDINGS IN THE IMPERFECT TENSE

–er	aprender	to learn (infinitive)
–ía	*(yo) aprendía*	I learned
–ías	*(tú) aprendías*	you learned (informal, singular)
–ía	*(él, ella) aprendía*	he, she, it learned
	(usted) aprendía	you learned (formal, singular)
–íamos	*(nosotros, nosotras) aprendíamos*	we learned
–íais	*(vosotros, vosotras) aprendíais*	you learned (informal, plural)
–ían	*(ellos, ellas) aprendían*	they learned
	(ustedes) aprendían	you learned (formal, plural)

▼ –*IR* VERB ENDINGS IN THE IMPERFECT TENSE

–*ir*	*vivir*	to live (infinitive)
–*ía*	*(yo) vivía*	I lived
–*ías*	*(tú) vivías*	you lived (informal, singular)
–*ía*	*(él, ella) vivía*	he, she, it lived
	(usted) vivía	you lived (formal, singular)
–*íamos*	*(nosotros, nosotras) vivíamos*	we lived
–*íais*	*(vosotros, vosotras) vivíais*	you lived (informal, plural)
–*ían*	*(ellos, ellas) vivían*	they lived
	(ustedes) vivían	you lived (formal, plural)

Preterite and Imperfect Together

It's not uncommon to combine the preterite and the imperfect verbs in the same sentence, especially with the words *de* and *cuando*. Take a look at the following examples:

A la vez que hacía la broma, sonrió.
As he was telling the joke, he smiled.

Ayer cuando caminaba al trabajo, vio un accidente.
Yesterday when he was walking to work, he saw an accident.

Nunca hablaba mal de otros, pero lo hizo hoy.
He never used to speak badly of others, but he did today.

For additional vocabulary words that will help you form similar sentences in the imperfect and preterite tenses, refer to the following table.

▼ VOCABULARY OFTEN USED WITH THE IMPERFECT AND PRETERITE TENSES

a la vez	at the same time
algunas veces	sometimes
a menudo	often
a veces	at times
cada día	each day, every day

contadas veces	seldom
de vez en cuando	once in a while
esta vez	this time
frecuentemente	frequently
muchas veces	many times
nunca	never
repetidamente	repeatedly
siempre	always
tantas veces	so many times
toda la semana	all week long
toda la vida	whole life

Alert

Take a look at the following two phrases: *cada mes* (each month) and *cada semana* (each week). Though *mes* is a masculine noun and *semana* is a feminine noun, the word *cada* does not change its ending. And, of course, it does not exist in the plural—"each" is always a singular idea.

Preterite Versus Imperfect

The preterite is a precise and limiting tense. The imperfect, on the other hand, is less restricted; it represents the vagueness of time with respect to the action. For a detailed review of when to use the preterite and the imperfect, refer to the following table.

▼ PRETERITE VERSUS IMPERFECT

Preterite	Imperfect
An act that occurs as a single event	An act that was customary in the past
An act limited in the times it is performed	An act that may be ongoing indefinitely
An act that is defined within specified time frames	An act that is defined within broad time frames

The following are some examples to help you differentiate between the imperfect and the preterite.

Ella fue al cine ayer.
She went to the movies yesterday.

De niña, ella iba al cine cada sábado.
As a young girl, she used to go to the movies every Saturday.

Me gustó la película.
I liked the movie.

A Jonathan le gustaba mucho el programa de televisión de Los Tres Chiflados.
Jonathan liked *The Three Stooges* television program very much.

La cita comenzó a las diez de la mañana.
The meeting began at ten in the morning.

De niños, comenzaban a llorar cada vez que oían el trueno.
As children, they used to begin to cry every time they heard thunder.

Present-Perfect Tense

The present-perfect tense is constructed by using a form of the auxiliary verb *haber* (to have) with the past-participle form of the primary verb. It characterizes a past connected to a now-expanded present. In a nutshell, the present-perfect tense is used to describe the following:

- **An immediate past.** For example: *No he comido porque acabo de llegar.* (I have not eaten because I have just arrived.)
- **A past inhabited by the speaker.** For example: *Últimamente, he tenido mucho sueño.* (Lately, I have been very sleepy.)
- **Information independent of time.** For example: *No he hablado con María.* (I haven't talked to Maria.)

- **A psychologically or emotionally linked past.** For example: *He perdido a mi abuelita hace diez años.* (I lost my grandma ten years ago.)

Conjugating Verbs in the Present-Perfect Tense

Present perfect is a composite tense—that is, the main verb *haber* (in this case the Spanish equivalent of the English verb "to have") is conjugated in the present tense and then matched with a past-participle form of another verb. So, conjugating verbs in this tense is really easy: All you need to know is how to conjugate *haber* and set the other verb as a past participle.

Let's start with *haber,* which is an irregular verb. Note that though it translates as "have" in the sense of "I have done . . . ," it is not used in the other sense of "have" (possession, ownership).

▼ **CONJUGATING *HABER* IN THE PRESENT TENSE**

(yo) he	I have
(tú) has	you have (informal, singular)
(él, ella, usted) ha	he, she, it has; you have (formal, singular)
(nosotros, nosotras) hemos	we have
(vosotros, vosotras) habéis	you have (informal, plural)
(ellos, ellas, ustedes) han	they have; you have (formal, plural)

Forming the past participle is even easier: If a verb ends in *–ar,* its corresponding past participle substitutes *–ar* with *–ado.* If it ends with *–er* or *–ir,* its corresponding past participle substitutes *–er* or *–ir* with *–ido.*

▼ **PRESENT PARTICIPLE CONJUGATIONS OF *CANTAR, APRENDER,* AND *VIVIR***

Pronoun	Cantar	Aprender	Vivir
yo	*he cantado*	*he aprendido*	*he vivido*
tú	*has cantado*	*has aprendido*	*has vivido*
él, ella, usted	*ha cantado*	*ha aprendido*	*ha vivido*
nosotros, nosotras	*hemos cantado*	*hemos aprendido*	*hemos vivido*
vosotros, vosotras	*habéis cantado*	*habéis aprendido*	*habéis vivido*

Pronoun	Cantar	Aprender	Vivir
ellos, ellas, ustedes	han cantado	han aprendido	han vivido

Future Tense

The future tense is just as easy to learn in Spanish as in English. What the future tense describes is fairly straightforward. The following types of actions are treated in the future tense:

- **Actions asserted as certain to occur within a period following the present.** For example: *Viajaré a Londres en septiembre.* (I will travel to London in September.)
- **Actions that will occur depending on uncertain but possible circumstances.** For example: *Comeré el almuerzo si tengo tiempo.* (I will eat lunch if I have time.)

Conjugating Verbs in the Future Tense

The endings for verbs in the future tense are the same for *–ar, –er,* and *–ir* verbs. However, there's a little trick you'll need to remember: You add the ending to the infinitive form *without* dropping the infinitive ending. The following table lists the conjugation endings, as well as examples.

▼ CONJUGATING VERBS IN THE FUTURE TENSE

Ending	Pronoun(s)	Cantar	Aprender	Vivir
–é	yo	cantaré	aprenderé	viviré
–ás	tú	cantarás	aprenderás	vivirás
–á	él, ella, usted	cantará	aprenderá	vivirá
–emos	nosotros, nosotras	cantaremos	aprenderemos	viviremos
–éis	vosotros, vosotras	cantaréis	aprenderéis	viviréis
–án	ellos, ellas, ustedes	cantarán	aprenderán	vivirán

Conditional Tense

The conditional tense in Spanish is generally equivalent to the English construction "would + verb." In Spanish, the conditional has five basic uses:

- **It roots a future action to the past.** For example: *Manuel me dijo que llegaría antes de las tres.* (Manuel told me that he would arrive before three.)
- **It allows for the hypothetical—with the implication that the conditional statement is unlikely.** For example: *Te compraría un pasaje a Europa, pero perdí todo el dinero en Las Vegas.* (I would buy you a trip to Europe, but I lost all my money in Las Vegas.)
- **It gives room for a probability that is more expansive and may include conjecture or approximation.** For example: *¿Con quién hablaría Juan a esas horas de la noche?* (With whom would Juan speak at that hour of night?)
- **It allows for a concession in light of a contrary view or experience introduced by *pero* (but).** For example: *Sería tacaño, pero nunca me negó su ayuda.* (He might have been stingy, but he never refused me his help.)
- **It provides an alternative to the copreterite in expressing a courteous request.** For example: *¿Podría decirme donde está la parada de autobús?* (Could you tell me where the bus stop is?)

The underlying idea to remember about the conditional is that the future is not so certain because what it depends on is either unlikely or too expansive to pin down and know readily.

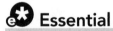 **Essential**

The conditional tense also appears in "if/then" constructions that are posed in the past tense. For instance, in English you would say, "If I had a dog, I would take care of it well." In Spanish, you would use the conditional for the "then" clause: *Si tuviera un perro, lo cuidaría bien.*

Conditional-Tense Conjugations

Conjugating verbs in the conditional tense is very easy, as long as you know the future-tense base. For regular verbs, that's simply the infinitive form, which you will use without dropping the –ar, –er, or –ir ending.

The conditional endings are the same for all three groups of verbs. For some examples, take a look at the following table:

▼ **CONJUGATING VERBS IN THE CONDITIONAL TENSE**

Ending	Pronoun(s)	Cantar	Aprender	Vivir
–ía	yo	cantaría	aprendería	viviría
–ías	tú	cantarías	aprenderías	vivirías
–ía	él, ella, usted	cantaría	aprendería	viviría
–íamos	nosotros, nosotras	cantaríamos	aprenderíamos	viviríamos
–íais	vosotros, vosotras	cantaríais	aprenderíais	viviríais
–ían	ellos, ellas, ustedes	cantarían	aprenderían	vivirían

Conjugating *Ser* and *Estar*

You already know how to conjugate regular verbs, but unfortunately not all Spanish verbs are regular. You have already learned the irregular present-tense verb forms for *ser* and *estar.* Now let's see how these verbs conjugate in the preterite, imperfect, present perfect, and future tenses (remember, you can use the future-tense base of the irregular verb to conjugate it in the conditional tense).

Preterite Tense

In the preterite, *ser* is used on "permanent" characteristics that nevertheless had a definite ending point—think of them as life-altering changes. *Estar* focuses on the situational and works better in describing a simple past that is at odds with the present. After all, a lot of things do in fact change, particularly situations. The action is still rooted in the past and cut off from the present, but the changes that may occur in the movement toward the present are more easily assigned to a discrete point in time rather than a continuum, as is the case with the imperfect tense.

Fui bajo.
I was short. (But now I'm tall.)

Ayer estuve cansado.
I was tired yesterday. (But I'm not tired anymore.)

Try to memorize the preterite conjugation forms of *ser* and *estar.*

▼ SER AND *ESTAR* IN THE PRETERITE TENSE

Pronoun(s)	Ser	Estar
yo	fui	estuve
tú	fuiste	estuviste
él, ella, usted	fue	estuvo
nosotros, nosotras	fuimos	estuvimos
vosotros, vosotras	fuisteis	estuvisteis
ellos, ellas, ustedes	fueron	estuvieron

Imperfect Tense

Estar, in the imperfect, describes continuous, habitual, or customary acts of "being" that coincide with the English "used to be" or "was (being)." For example:

Estaba en el jardín cuando llegó el sol.
I was in the garden when the sun came.

The preterite and the imperfect can actually coincide. That is, the preterite can be contained within a time frame established by the copreterite, as in:

Ayer mientras estaba en el trabajo, hablé con Luisa.
Yesterday while I was at work, I talked to Luisa.

With regard to *ser*, the imperfect tense may describe habitual or customary acts of "being" that coincide with the English "used to be" during a fairly vague period of time. It is often employed to complete the phrase "When I was . . ."

Cuando era niño, era travieso.
When I was a boy, I was mischievous.

Cuando era adolescente, era buena estudiante.
When she was an adolescent, she was a good student.

Notice that these time frames are common to everyone. You've also been a child and an adolescent at one time or another. Because the imperfect makes no reference to something having ended, it is often used to render descriptions of personal characteristics by relying on the preposition *de*. You can say:

De joven, era audaz.
When I was young, I was audacious.

De soltera, era demasiado seria.
When I was single, I was too serious.

De casado, era tranquilo.
When I was married, I was calm.

For conjugated forms of *ser* and *estar* in the imperfect, refer to the following table.

▼ *SER* AND *ESTAR* IN THE IMPERFECT TENSE

Pronoun(s)	Ser	Estar
yo	*era*	*estaba*
tú	*eras*	*estabas*
él, ella, usted	*era*	*estaba*
nosotros, nosotras	*éramos*	*estábamos*

Pronoun(s)	Ser	Estar
vosotros, vosotras	erais	estabais
ellos, ellas, ustedes	eran	estaban

Present-Perfect Tense

In this tense, *ser* and *estar* both translate to "have been." As you might remember, the conjugations are constructed by using a form of the auxiliary verb *haber* ("to have") with the past participle (or *–do*) form of the primary verb: in this case, *sido* and *estado*. For example:

Durante mi vida he sido estudiante, marinero, y vendedor de zapatos.
During my life I've been a student, sailor, and shoe seller.

He estado aquí dos horas.
I have been here for two hours.

He estado con resfriado desde ayer.
I have had a cold since yesterday.

Future Tense

Despite offering the present tense to describe future events, Spanish also has its own strictly future-focused tense.

La semana próxima estaré en Buenos Aires.
Next week I will be in Buenos Aires.

Qué será, será.
What will be, will be.

The following table contains the conjugations of *ser* and *estar* in the future tense.

▼ **SER** AND **ESTAR** IN THE FUTURE TENSE

Pronoun(s)	Ser	Estar
yo	*seré*	*estaré*
tú	*serás*	*estarás*
él, ella, usted	*será*	*estará*
nosotros, nosotras	*seremos*	*estaremos*
vosotros, vosotras	*seréis*	*estaréis*
ellos, ellas, ustedes	*serán*	*estarán*

CHAPTER 8

The Vocabulary of Time

Regardless of how many grammatical tenses a language boasts, when it comes to the concept of time there are really only three general frames of reference—past, present, and future—by which to witness daily life. Measuring and telling time is an important part of learning Spanish—and a good way for you to practice your verb tenses!

Cardinal Numbers

Spanish employs cardinal and ordinal numerals (as does English). You are probably more familiar with the cardinals—numerals that express quantity and are used for counting: one, two, three, and so on. In fact, Spanish often uses cardinal numerals even when American English would choose ordinals—numerals that show the order of an item in a given series: first, second, third, and so on.

The Basics: 0–15

The single-digit numbers 1 through 9 are the most utilized in Spanish because they are employed alone *and* within larger numbers. All you really need to do is memorize the first nine, plus the word for 0 and 10 through 15; the rest is a matter of combining what you already know. When simply counting, numerals stand alone. Treat them as you would pronouns:

0	cero	8	ocho
1	uno	9	nueve
2	dos	10	diez
3	tres	11	once
4	cuatro	12	doce
5	cinco	13	trece
6	seis	14	catorce
7	siete	15	quince

When enumerating items, however, the numeral is acting as an adjective and precedes the items enumerated. Any number above *uno* requires the use of the plural form of the item. Keep in mind that the actual numeral employed will not be in the plural form for quantities less than 200. For example:

un sacerdote	one priest
una bebida	one drink
cinco dedos	five fingers
cinco quejas	five complaints
ocho vestidos	eight dresses
ocho cortinas	eight curtains

 Fact

The cardinal number as a preceding adjective often enumerates the quantity of items. When the cardinal number follows the item(s), it is limiting the discussion to the item in the position described by the number. For example: *cinco volúmenes* (five volumes), as opposed to *volumen cinco* (volume five).

Moving On: 16–99

Double-digit numbers are formed similarly to the way they are formed in English. For example, "21" is "twenty-one." If you know the words for "twenty," "thirty," "forty," and so on, as well as how to count from 1 to 9, you will be able to come up with any number from 1 to 100.

It is pretty much the same in Spanish. First, you need to learn the numbers divisible by 10:

10	diez	60	sesenta
20	veinte	70	setenta
30	treinta	80	ochenta
40	cuarenta	90	noventa
50	cincuenta		

The rules are slightly different for numbers 16 through 29 than for 30 through 99. Take a look at how the numbers 16 through 29 are formed:

16	diez y seis	dieciséis	23	veinte y tres	veintitrés
17	diez y siete	diecisiete	24	veinte y cuatro	veinticuatro
18	diez y ocho	dieciocho	25	veinte y cinco	veinticinco
19	diez y nueve	diecinueve	26	veinte y seis	veintiséis
20	veinte		27	veinte y siete	veintisiete
21	veinte y uno	veintiuno	28	veinte y ocho	veintiocho
22	veinte y dos	veintidós	29	veinte y nueve	veintinueve

For numbers 30 through 99, the rule is exactly the same, and there is no need to combine the number into one word: The two components remain connected by a y (and). Here are a few examples:

36	treinta y seis
48	cuarenta y ocho
59	cincuenta y nueve
81	ochenta y uno

Next Up: Hundreds

In Spanish, you rarely if ever say "one hundred"—instead, you simply say cien (hundred). Any number between 101 and 199 uses the term *ciento* in combination with the numerals specified in the previous section. Notice that a conjunction is not used between the "hundred" and "ten" words:

116	*ciento dieciséis*
131	*ciento treinta y uno*
177	*ciento setenta y siete*

Multiples of 100 are *cientos*. To create a specific number of "hundred" units, all you really need to do is combine the number of 100s with *cientos*:

200	*doscientos*	600	*seiscientos*
300	*trescientos*	700	*setecientos*
400	*cuatrocientos*	800	*ochocientos*
500	*quinientos*	900	*novecientos*

🅴❗ Alert

Notice that the words for 500, 700, and 900 do not follow the regular numeral + *cientos* pattern. To review, they are: *quinientos* (500), *setecientos* (700), and *novecientos* (900).

It follows, then, that for numbers 201 to 999, the process for putting together the numbers goes like this:

206	*doscientos seis*
331	*trescientos treinta y uno*
447	*cuatrocientos cuarenta y siete*
650	*seiscientos cincuenta*
809	*ochocientos nueve*

Keep in mind: You should use *y* only between the "tens" and the "units" values. Otherwise, the *y* is omitted (so, *treinta y ocho,* but *trescientos ochenta*). Also, the numbers containing "hundreds" parts do conform to the gender of the nouns they modify. For example: *trescientas casas* (300 homes), *quinientas veintiuna quejas* (521 complaints).

Moreover: Thousands

Like *cien, mil* (thousand) generally exists without a preceding article. Unlike *ciento,* however, *mil* does not take on any endings when it is part of a number. For any number of thousands above 1,000, simply place the number of thousands before *mil (dos mil, tres mil,* and so on). For example:

1,216	*mil doscientos dieciséis*
2,331	*dos mil trescientos treinta y uno*
3,477	*tres mil cuatrocientos setenta y siete*
5,000	*cinco mil*
45,783	*cuarenta y cinco mil setecientos ochenta y tres*

 **Essential**

Spanish provides two equivalent constructions to express the collective noun "thousands"—*miles de* + noun or *millares de* + noun. For example: *Miles de personas votan. Millares de personas votan.* (Thousands of people vote.) Preference for one expression over the other is largely a regional issue.

Note that when you write in Spanish, you use a period instead of a comma to separate the digits in numbers greater than 1,000, and vice versa for the sign used to denote decimal points. For example, in Spanish, you would write 3.000 for the English 3,000, and 4,7 for the English 4.7.

Millions and Beyond

This is a time to recall the warning on misleading cognates from the first chapter. Though some Spanish and American English numbers do coincide (like million and *millón*), larger numbers do not. Compare:

millón	million
mil millones	billion
billón	trillion

Use the following examples to practice what you have just learned.

1,000,001	*un millón uno*
2,000,002	*dos millones dos*
1,000,000,345	*mil millones, trescientos cuarenta y cinco*
14,500,900,005	*catorce mil millones, quinientos millones, novecientos mil, cinco*
1,000,100,700,000	*un billón, cien millones, setecientos mil*

 Fact

With regard to the use of a number as an adjective or a noun, *de* is inserted between a specific number and the accompanying items only for numbers specified to the nearest (whole) million and above. For example: *dos millones de pesos* (two million pesos), but *dos millones tres pesos* (two million and three pesos).

A subtle change in meaning occurs when you begin using numbers in the millions and larger. You already know that "hundreds" and "thousands" no longer describe the quantity of things, but that they themselves become the objects of discussion. This is generally true of one million and beyond. Whereas you can say *cien mujeres* (100 women), you cannot say *un millón mujeres*—the correct phrase would be *un millón de mujeres* (one million women), where *de mujeres* describes the million. If you are talking of an unspecified number of books ranging in the millions, then you would say *millones de libros*.

Ordinal Numbers

When ordinal numbers describe a noun's position in a series, they act as adjectives and generally come before the noun they are modifying. Unlike cardinal numbers, ordinal numbers correspond in gender and number with the noun they describe. For example:

el primer día
the first day

la primera semana
the first week

los primeros días
the first days

las primeras semanas
the first weeks

On its own, an ordinal may express a "position" as a place rather than a description, as in this sentence:

Yo salí de la casa primero.
I left the house first.

The following table presents ordinal numbers. Unless otherwise noted, this general form is the same as the masculine singular form.

▼ **CARDINAL NUMBERS**

primer, primero	first	octavo	eighth
segundo	second	noveno	ninth
tercer, tercero	third	décimo	tenth

cuarto	fourth	undécimo	eleventh
quinto	fifth	duodécimo	twelfth
sexto	sixth	decimotercero	thirteenth
séptimo	seventh	decimocuarto	fourteenth

Recall what happens to *uno* when used to describe quantity with respect to a masculine noun. As you might remember, "one car" in Spanish would be translated as *un coche*. That is, *uno* loses the final *–o* before a masculine noun. The same is true with the ordinals *primero* and *tercero* when they precede the noun they modify. For example: *el primer coche* (the first car) and *el decimotercer coche* (the thirteenth car).

Days of the Week

To help you review the ordinal numbers, how about learning the days of the week? The following list answers the question *¿Cuáles son los días de la semana?* (What are the days of the week?). For a list of days of the week, refer to the table that follows.

El lunes es el primer día de la semana.
Monday is the first day of the week.

El martes es el segundo día de la semana.
Tuesday is the second day of the week.

El miércoles es el tercer día de la semana.
Wednesday is the third day of the week.

El jueves es el cuarto día de la semana.
Thursday is the fourth day of the week.

El viernes es el quinto día de la semana.
Friday is the fifth day of the week.

El sábado es el sexto día de la semana.
Saturday is the sixth day of the week.

El domingo es el séptimo día de la semana.
Sunday is the seventh day of the week.

▼ DAYS OF THE WEEK

lunes	Monday
martes	Tuesday
miércoles	Wednesday
jueves	Thursday
viernes	Friday
sábado	Saturday
domingo	Sunday

Other words that will help you set the sentence in the correct time frame include the following (listed in chronological order):

▼ TIME VOCABULARY

el año pasado	last year
la semana pasada	last week
anteayer	day before yesterday
ayer	yesterday
este año	this year
esta semana	this week
hoy	today
mañana	tomorrow
pasado mañana	day after tomorrow
la semana próxima	next week
el próximo año	next year

The following set of examples illustrates how these vocabulary words work within the Spanish sentence:

Esta semana he estado enfermo con un resfriado.
This week I have been sick with a cold.

Toda la semana pasada, estuve de vacaciones.
I was on vacation all last week.

Estaré en las Islas Galápagos la semana próxima.
I will be in the Galápagos Islands next week.

Este año, tendré un empleo nuevo.
This year, I will have a new job.

El año pasado, estaba en Santo Domingo.
Last year, I was in Santo Domingo.

El próximo año, estaré en Madrid.
Next year, I will be in Madrid.

 **Essential**

To use *ser* in expressing time and days of the week, follow the format of the following question and answer: *¿Qué día es hoy?* (What day is it today?) *Hoy es lunes.* (Today is Monday.) Consequently, you would say *mañana es martes, en dos días es miércoles, en tres días es jueves,* and so on.

You know how to say what day it is, but what about the date? In Spanish, the date is known as *la fecha: ¿Cuál es la fecha de hoy?* (Which is the date today?) *Hoy es lunes, el catorce de junio.* (Today is Monday, June 14.) *De hoy en ocho días, es martes, el veintidos de junio.* (Eight days from today, it is Tuesday, June 22.)

The Months and Seasons

Moving on from days of the week, let's look at the months of the year and the four seasons. The list of *los meses* (the months) in Spanish appears in the following table.

▼ **MONTHS OF THE YEAR**

enero	January
febrero	February
marzo	March
abril	April
mayo	May
junio	June
julio	July
agosto	August
septiembre	September
octubre	October
noviembre	November
diciembre	December

There is a slight difference in handling days, seasons, and months. Unless replaced by other modifiers such as "each," a definite article precedes days and seasons: *el lunes* (Monday), *la primavera* (spring). However, months are only specified by the definite article when speaking about a specific time when an event occurred or will occur: *en enero* (in January).

In Spanish, the four seasons of the year correspond to the English winter, spring, summer, and fall. The seasons are listed in the following table.

▼ **SEASONS OF THE YEAR**

el invierno	winter
la primavera	spring
el verano	summer
el otoño	autumn, fall

Asking and Telling Time

What time is it? It's a common enough question. In Spanish, the word *tiempo* refers to the general concept of "time," as in *Tengo tiempo ahora* ("I have time now"). Curiously enough, it also means "weather." So if you ask someone ¿*Qué tiempo hace?* "What's the weather like?" the person will give you a weather report, not the current time. You will be better served by thinking in terms *la hora*, "the hour." The most common ways to ask the time are the following phrases:

¿Qué hora es?

¿Qué horas son?

 Alert

It should be noted that the most educated way of asking the time in Spanish is to use the singular "*¿Qué hora es?*" according to the *RAE* (*Real Academia Española*), the Spanish institution responsible for enforcing grammatical unity. However, the plural version "*Qué horas son?*" is very common, especially in Mexico, the Dominican Republic, and Puerto Rico.

The plural *son* is not recommended by the grammarians, but it is accepted and used mostly informally by the people. As far as the response to the question, native speakers may employ the singular or the plural, depending on the actual time. The possible responses may be:

Es la una.
It's one o'clock.

Son las dos.
It's two o'clock.

Son las once.
It's eleven o'clock.

Son las doce en punto.
It's twelve o'clock on the dot.

Fact

In Spain and Latin American countries, time is generally noted with respect to a twenty-four-hour clock (particularly in written form). Depending on the country, you may see 2 P.M. written as 1400, 14h00m, 14:00, or 14'00; and 2:30 A.M. may be written as 02.30, 02h30m, 02:30, or 02'30.

In actual conversation, the hour is treated much as in English—it is differentiated by the part of the day:

Spanish	English	When to Use
de la madrugada	in the early morning	until dawn
de la mañana	in the morning	until noon
de la tarde	in the afternoon/in the evening	before sunset
de la noche	at night	after sunset until midnight

Here are some examples:

Son las dos de la madrugada.
It's two in the early morning.

Son las seis de la mañana.
It's six in the morning.

Son las dos de la tarde.
It's two in the afternoon.

Son las diez de la noche.
It's ten at night.

But what are the chances that the time will be exactly six or two or ten? To express minutes, these rules would apply:

• Minutes 1 through 30 are "added" to *la hora.*

- Minutes 31 through 59 are "subtracted" from *la hora* with *menos* (minus).
- You can also tell time by dividing the hour in half (*media*) and in quarters (*cuartos*).

For example:

1:23 P.M.	*la una y veintitrés de la tarde*
9:17 P.M.	*las nueve y diecisiete de la noche*
12:40 A.M.	*la una menos veinte de la mañana*
5:50 A.M.	*las seis menos diez de la mañana*
13:15 P.M.	*la una y cuarto de la tarde*
1:30 A.M.	*la una y media de la madrugada*
13:45 P.M.	*las dos menos cuarto de la tarde*

Additional vocabulary words to help answer the question *¿A qué hora . . . ?* (At what time . . . ?) are listed in the following table.

▼ ADDITIONAL VOCABULARY FOR TELLING TIME

el mediodía	noon
por la mañana	in the morning
la madrugada	early morning, dawn
por la tarde	in the afternoon/evening
la medianoche	midnight
por la noche	in the night

Though a standard does exist for telling time, nonstandard ways of doing so have taken hold in some areas, particularly in the United States. It's not that these ways are wrong—it's just that they are not widely employed. Here are some you might encounter:

¿Tiene la hora? or *¿Tiene hora?*
Do you have the time?

Son las seis y quince.
It's six fifteen.

Son las siete y cincuenta y cinco.
It's seven fifty-five.

Faltan diez para las tres.
Ten minutes remain before three.

CHAPTER 9

Important Verbs to Know

The Spanish language has a plethora of verbs—some are regular in all their conjugations, and others have various irregularities. This chapter will examine a few irregular verbs that are frequently found in the Spanish sentence. These verbs are connected with concepts that are important to learn, and will help you master other areas of the Spanish language as you examine each one.

To Have and to Have To: *Tener*

It is now time to meet *tener*, one of those verbs it's hard to get along without. *Tener* corresponds to descriptions of experience. In its simplest form, it means "to have." To learn how to conjugate *tener* in the present tense, refer to the following table.

▼ CONJUGATING *TENER* IN THE PRESENT TENSE

yo tengo	I have
tú tienes	you have (informal, singular)
él, ella, usted tiene	he, she, it has; you have (formal, singular)
nosotros, nosotras tenemos	we have
vosotros, vosotras tenéis	you have (informal, plural)
ellos, ellas, ustedes tienen	they have, you have (formal, plural)

Tengo un coche rojo.
I have a red car.

Marisela tiene un paraguas azul.
Marisela has a blue umbrella.

¿Cuántos años tiene usted?
How old are you?

Experience with *Tener*

Tener may also be used in expressions where it means something like "to be," physically, mentally, or emotionally. This means that, oddly enough, *tener* may appear in many of the same situations as the *estar con* combination. Take a look at the following table.

▼ *TENER* USED AS "TO BE"

Spanish	Literally	English
Tengo celos.	I am (experiencing) jealousy.	I am jealous.
Tengo fiebre.	I am (experiencing) fever.	I am feverish.
Tengo frío.	I am (experiencing) cold.	I am cold.
Tengo hambre.	I am (experiencing) hunger.	I am hungry.
Tengo miedo.	I am (experiencing) fear.	I am afraid.
Tengo sed.	I am (experiencing) thirst.	I am thirsty.
Tengo sueño.	I am (experiencing) sleepiness.	I am sleepy.
Tengo vergüenza.	I am (experiencing) shame.	I am embarrassed.

To be more specific, you can then add modifiers to clarify what you are experiencing. Pick one of two modifiers—*mucho* (much, many) or *poco* (little, few). Remember: The modifiers must adopt the gender and number of the condition.

▼ *¿MUCHO O POCO?* (MANY OR FEW?)

Tengo miedo.	*Tengo mucho miedo.*	*Tengo poco miedo.*
Tengo sed.	*Tengo mucha sed.*	*Tengo poca sed.*
Tengo celos.	*Tengo muchos celos.*	*Tengo pocos celos.*

But there's more. Take a look at the following examples, which also rely on the verb *tener*:

Tengo cuidado.	I am careful.
Tengo la culpa.	I am at fault.
Tengo éxito.	I am successful; I have success.
Tengo quince años.	I am fifteen years old; I have reached fifteen years.
Tengo razón.	I am in the right; I am right.
Tengo suerte.	I am lucky; I have luck.

An Infinitive Construction: *Tener Que*

Up to this point you've seen the infinitive only as a point of reference to determine meaning and conjugation. You may recall that the infinitive also allows you to speak of an action without really needing to make it active or attribute it to an actor. For example:

Aprendo a nadar.
I am learning to swim.

An interesting manifestation of this use of the infinitive can be seen in the expression of obligation that is created when *tener* combines with *que* ("what/that," though not translated in this situation) and the infinitive. In this case, the *tener que* construction may be translated as "have to" or "has to":

Tengo que ir a casa.
I have to go home.

Conjugating *Tener* Through the Spanish Tenses

In the preterite tense, *tener* describes an experience, or sensation, that is known to have ended and, as a result, is tied only to the past, often as a single event. For example:

Anoche tuve poca hambre.
I was not very hungry last night.

Notice that the conjugations do not follow the regular –er verb rules. The base changes to *tuv*– and the endings are slightly different as well. Refer to the following table for the irregular preterite conjugations of *tener*.

▼ CONJUGATING *TENER* IN PRETERITE TENSE

yo tuve	I had
tú tuviste	you had (informal, singular)
él, ella, usted tuvo	he, she, it had; you had (formal, singular)
nosotros, nosotras tuvimos	we had
vosotros, vosotras tuvisteis	you had
ellos, ellas, ustedes tuvieron	they had, you had (plural)

Luckily, *tener* follows regular verb rules in the imperfect tense. The imperfect is characterized by its ongoing development in the past, rather than by its termination, which is vague. Here are a few examples with respect to the imperfect form of *tener:*

Hace muchos años, tenía una mascota.
Several years ago, I had a pet.

As you may remember, the present-perfect tense characterizes an experience as having occurred in the recent past:

He tenido sueño todo el día.
I have been sleepy all day.

Finally, in the the future tense, *tener* describes a future state, bound or unbound by reference to time. Note that while the endings for conjugating *tener* in the future tense are regular, the base is not *tener*– but *tendr*–.
For example:

Tendré treinta y seis años en julio.
I will be thirty-six years old in July.

Haber: To Have or to Be?

This verb should be familiar to you—it is the auxiliary verb "to have" that you've been introduced to when learning about the present-perfect tense.

He sido plomero.
I have been a plumber.

However, *haber* can be found in other types of constructions as well. One of the most common usages for this verb is in the "impersonal third-person" present-tense form *hay*. Because it is used as both singular and plural, it may be translated as either "there is" or "there are," depending on the context. As such, it may be used to:

1. Ask questions characterized by existence:

   ¿Hay alguién aquí?
   Is there someone here?

2. State the existence of something:

   Hay pan fresco en la cocina.
   There is fresh bread in the kitchen.

3. State a broad "impersonal" obligation (lacking a specific subject, sometimes translated into English as "one") in the form of *hay + que + infinitive*:

   Hay que luchar por la vida.
   One must fight for one's life.

There are two important distinctions to be made regarding *hay* and other verbs with similar uses. First, there is a tendency to confuse *hay* with forms of *estar*. It is best to distinguish them by noting that whereas *estar* expresses the position or location of someone or something, *hay* refers to that someone's or something's very existence. Compare:

Está en casa.
He is at home.

Hay alguien en casa.
There is someone at home.

Second, there is also a tendency to confuse *hay* with *tener* within a *tener que* + infinitive phrase. Remember that while both express an obligation, *tener que* . . . has a specific subject (and *tener* is conjugated according to that subject), whereas the *hay que* . . . construction expresses an obligation not specifically assigned to a particular individual. Compare:

Hay que comprarlo.
Someone should buy it.

Tengo que comprarlo.
I have to buy it.

Other Uses and Applications of *Haber*

As an auxiliary verb, *haber* plays an important role in forming compound tenses. Though these tenses are really beyond the scope of this book, here's a short preview of what to expect.

When it comes to verb tenses, recall that a completed action is described as being "perfect." This being the case, you will often find a form of *haber* helping the past participle of a verb achieve this completion. You've already seen this occur in the present perfect, where *haber* is conjugated in the present tense to bring the completed action of a recent past into closer focus by means of the present. For example:

Yo he terminado el trabajo.
I have finished the work.

¿Te has duchado ya?
Have you already showered?

In the past-perfect (or pluperfect) tense, the past participle remains but *haber* is conjugated in the imperfect.

▼ *HABER* CONJUGATED IN THE IMPERFECT TENSE

yo había
tú habías
él, ella, usted había
nosotros, nosotras habíamos
vosotros, vosotras habíais
ellos, ellas, ustedes habían

The key to understanding this tense is the use of "had" in its translation. The focus on completed action is now shifted from the present back to the past. For example:

Yo ya había terminado el trabajo.
I had already finished the work.

¿Te habías duchado ya?
Had you already showered?

Similarly, *haber* also appears in the future-perfect tense.

▼ *HABER* IN THE FUTURE-PERFECT TENSE

yo habré
tú habrás
él, ella, usted habrá
nosotros, nosotras habremos
vosotros, vosotras habréis
ellos, ellas, ustedes habrán

This compound tense is used in two situations:

1. To describe an action as something that "will have" occurred by a deadline of sorts:

   Yo habré terminado el trabajo para las dos.
   I will have finished the work by two.

2. To describe an action as something that "must have" occurred, though there is a very slight chance that it hasn't:

   Me habré equivocado.
   I must have been mistaken.

The last compound tense in the indicative mood is the conditional perfect. This tense is the hardest to grasp because the focus of the completed action is not a single point in time but a continuum. See the following table for conditional-tense conjugations of *haber.*

▼ *HABER* CONJUGATED IN THE CONDITIONAL-PERFECT TENSE

yo habría
tú habrías
él, ella, usted habría
nosotros, nosotras habríamos
vosotros, vosotras habríais
ellos, ellas, ustedes habrían

There are three uses for the conditional perfect. They include:

1. Expressing a future action sandwiched between two events:

   Usted me aseguró que habría pintado la casa antes de entregármela.
   You assured me that you would have painted the house before giving it to me.

2. Expressing an action that failed because of some hindrance:

Yo habría terminado el trabajo, pero no tenía las herramientas adecuadas.
I would have finished the work, but I did not have the appropriate tools.

3. Expressing an expansive past probability, allowing for conjecture or approximation.

If someone were to ask, "Why is Tom not in his office?" one possible response is, "He must have become ill" (the future perfect). But if the question was posed as a past event, "Why was Tom not in his office?" a possible response to is, "He must have been ill" (conditional perfect; *se habría enfermado*). Remember: Both responses express probabilities, but the former forms a conjecture that begins in the future, and the latter forms one rooted in the past.

To Finish: *Acabar*

You will discover that in addition to *tener* and *haber*, there is a multitude of expressions that can be gotten from only a few simple words. And, as you have seen with *estar*, prepositions can make quite a significant addition to a verb. Take the word *acabar* (to finish). In its most basic form, it conjugates as a regular *–ar* verb.

▼ **CONJUGATING *ACABAR* IN THE PRESENT TENSE**

yo acabo	I finish
tú acabas	you finish (informal, singular)
él, ella, usted acaba	he, she finishes; you finish (formal, singular)
nosotros, nosotras acabamos	we finish
vosotros, vosotras acabais	you finish (informal, plural)
ellos, ellas, ustedes acaban	they finish; you finish (formal, plural)

By itself, *acabar* is used exactly as you would expect:

Hoy acabo la tarea.
Today I finish the homework.

It also conjugates as a regular *–ar* verb in other tenses, such as the imperfect and the future (see the following examples):

Raúl acabará sus vacaciones la semana próxima.
Raul will be finishing his vacation next week.

When combined with the preposition *con* (with), *acabar* is used in the sense of "to destroy," "to finish off," or "to break."

Mañana acabo con todo.
Tomorrow I will finish off everything.

In Conversation

In conversation, *acabar* often appears in combination with *de* + infinitive, such as in the following sentences:

Acabamos de nadar.
We have just finished swimming.

Notice that this construction requires you to use the present tense to consider a recent action performed to its end. Though you will find the *acabar de* + *infinitivo* in other tenses, the immediacy related to a completed act is only apparent within the present and imperfect tenses, where the conjugated action itself is considered in midstate. Key to understanding the *acabar de* + *infinitivo* construction in the imperfect is that it describes the period soon after an action was completed as a setting for something else to occur. For example:

Acabábamos de nadar.
We had just finished swimming.

To Go: *Ir*

As you've already seen with *tener, haber,* and *acabar,* the right combination of verb and preposition can add significantly to your expressive potential. The next verb introduced in this chapter will further enhance this potential to an astounding degree. *Ir* is among the most useful, most versatile, and most difficult verbs to master, but your command of this verb will serve you well. Its meaning is simple—"to go"—but as in English, its reach goes farther than the two letters would suggest.

Ir is one of the few "innately" irregular verbs—its irregularities are specific to itself and have simply evolved without pronunciation concerns. Take a look at its different tenses and see how the verb changes across time.

▼ CONJUGATING *IR* IN THE PRESENT, PRETERITE, IMPERFECT, AND FUTURE TENSES

Pronoun	Present	Preterite	Imperfect	Future
yo	*voy*	*fui*	*iba*	*iré*
tú	*vas*	*fuiste*	*ibas*	*irás*
él, ella, usted	*va*	*fue*	*iba*	*irá*
nosotros, nosotras	*vamos*	*fuimos*	*íbamos*	*iremos*
vosotros, vosotras	*vais*	*fuisteis*	*ibais*	*iréis*
ellos, ellas, ustedes	*van*	*fueron*	*iban*	*irán*

 Fact

As you might remember, the present-perfect tense is formed with the conjugation of the verb *haber* and the past-participle form of the main verb. The past participle of *ir* is *ido*. You will see examples of *ir* in the present-perfect tense among the sample sentences that follow.

A significant step in understanding how *ir* is used involves coming to the realization that "to go" requires direction. Take a look at the following sentences:

¿Vas a la carnicería?
Are you going to the butcher shop?

Ellas van a la sinagoga.
They go to the synagogue.

Mauricio fue a la boda de su mejor amigo.
Mauricio went to his best friend's wedding.

¿Adónde fuiste ayer?
Where did you go yesterday?

Marta iba a las fiestas de la escuela.
Marta used to go to the school parties.

He ido a varios conciertos.
I have gone to various concerts.

¿Has ido al Japón?
Have you gone to Japan?

¿Irás al cine el sábado?
Will you go to the movies on Saturday?

Van a ser las dos de la tarde.
It is going to be two in the afternoon.

An important construction to keep in mind is *ir a + infinitivo*. With it you can describe an immediate future (the beginning of an action) or an intention. In English, the equivalent construction is "to be going to." For example:

Voy a comprar una bicicleta.
I am going to buy a bicycle.

Voy a comer un bistec.
I am going to eat a steak.

Iban a visitar el museo.
They were going to visit the museum.

To Know: *Saber* and *Conocer*

By now you've undoubtedly noticed how subtle the differences between words can be. You've experienced "to be" in the forms of *ser, estar, tener,* and *hacer.* You'll be glad to know that as soon as you master those words, there are several others to challenge your curiosity—and the Spanish words meaning "to know" are among them.

The idea of "knowing" in Spanish is divided between two words—*saber* and *conocer.* Take a look at their present-tense conjugations in the following table.

▼ CONJUGATING *SABER* AND *CONOCER* IN THE PRESENT TENSE

Pronoun	Saber	Conocer
yo	*sé*	*conozco*
tú	*sabes*	*conoces*
él, ella, usted	*sabe*	*conoce*
nosotros, nosotras	*sabemos*	*conocemos*
vosotros, vosotras	*sabéis*	*conocéis*
ellos, ellas, ustedes	*saben*	*conocen*

Although both *saber* and *conocer* may be translated as "to know," they deal with different concepts. *Saber* conveys knowledge of a fact or a skill, and *conocer* conveys familiarity, be it with people, places, or things. These differences are outlined in the following table.

Saber	Conocer
to know that . . .	to be acquainted with, or well versed in . . .
to know facts	to know people
to know information	to be familiar with places and things

To review, compare the following pairs:

Yo sé como llegar a tu casa.
I know how to arrive at your house.

Yo conozco la ruta a tu casa.
I know the route to your house.

Ella no sabe quien llamó.
She doesn't know who called. (She doesn't have that information.)

Ella no la conoce.
She doesn't know her.

Constructions with *Saber*

Here are a few constructions with *saber* that are useful to know:
Saber + *Que* (To Know That)

Sé que la casa está lejos de aquí.
I know that the house is far from here.

Lorena sabe que Juan es buena persona.
Lorena knows that Juan is a good person.

Saber + Infinitivo (To Know How To)

¿Sabes nadar?
Do you know how to swim?

No sabemos patinar.
We don't know how to skate.

CHAPTER 10

Present-Tense Irregular Verbs

Not all verbs fit the regular-verb molds you've learned so far (*ser*, *estar*, *tener*, and *haber* are among the irregular verbs you already know). When you conjugate irregular verbs, you need to know how their bases change in various conjugations. This chapter will introduce you to verbs that are irregular in the present tense.

What's the Explanation?

For one reason or another, irregular verbs cannot keep their infinitive bases in some or all of their conjugated forms. What are the reasons behind these irregularities? Some irregularities are actually "regular"; that is, the changes that verbs undergo run consistently across verb groups. You will see that group irregularities also depend on similar letter substitutions.

Some irregularities result from spelling accommodations describing changes that occur to keep pronunciation consistent. A few verbs are "naturally" irregular. Most often, these are words that have been present in Spanish for a long time and have changed radically over centuries; *ser* is a good example—it is irregular in most of its conjugated forms. Fortunately, only a small fraction of all Spanish verbs are irregular.

▼ IRREGULAR VERBS

andar	to walk	*poder*	to be able to
asir	to seize	*poner*	to place, to put
caber	to fit	*producir*	to produce
caer	to fall	*querer*	to want, to love
dar	to give	*saber*	to know
decir	to say	*salir*	to leave
haber	to have, to be	*traer*	to bring
hacer	to do, to make	*valer*	to be worth
ir	to go	*venir*	to come
oír	to hear	*ver*	to see

 Essential

As you learn each verb, check to see whether it is regular or irregular. If it happens to be irregular, try to see if its irregularity is the same as that of another verb you are already familiar with—then, all you'll need to do is memorize how to conjugate one irregular verb instead of two. For example, did you know that *estar* and *tener* behave similarly in the preterite tense?

Reviewing What You Already Know

The present-tense verbs are formed by dropping their infinitive endings, –*ar*, –*er*, or –*ir*, and adding appropriate endings based on the person and number of the verb's subject. The following three tables list the present-tense verb endings for your review.

▼ REGULAR –*AR* VERBS

Pronoun	Ending	Sample Verb Conjugation
	–*ar*	*ganar* (to win, earn)
yo	–*o*	*gano*
tú	–*as*	*ganas*
él, ella, usted	–*a*	*gana*
nosotros, nosotras	–*amos*	*ganamos*

Pronoun	Ending	Sample Verb Conjugation
vosotros, vosotras	–áis	ganáis
ellos, ellas, ustedes	–an	ganan

▼ REGULAR –ER VERBS

Pronoun	Ending	Sample Verb Conjugation
	–er	beber (to drink)
yo	–o	bebo
tú	–es	bebes
él, ella, usted	–e	bebe
nosotros, nosotras	–emos	bebemos
vosotros, vosotras	–éis	bebéis
ellos, ellas, ustedes	–en	beben

▼ REGULAR –IR VERBS

Pronoun	Ending	Sample Verb Conjugation
	–ir	recibir (to receive)
yo	–o	recibo
tú	–es	recibes
él, ella, usted	–e	recibe
nosotros, nosotras	–imos	recibimos
vosotros, vosotras	–ís	recibís
ellos, ellas, ustedes	–en	reciben

Group Irregularities

Group irregularities (that is, irregularities that occur in patterns, among certain groups of verbs) generally result from vowel-focused modifications. Letter substitutions often occur across person and number, without affecting the employment of the regular verb endings.

Let's take a look at the first type of group irregularity, a diphthong base change from *e* to *ie*. This change occurs with many irregular verbs, across all three conjugation groups (among *ar*, *er*, and *ir* verbs). As an example, take a look at how to conjugate *calentar* (to heat).

▼ DIPHTHONG BASE CHANGE FROM *E* TO *IE*

	−ar	*calentar* (to heat)
yo	−o	*caliento*
tú	−as	*calientas*
él, ella, usted	−a	*calienta*
nosotros, nosotras	−amos	*calentamos*
vosotros, vosotras	−áis	*calentáis*
ellos, ellas, ustedes	−an	*calientan*

 Fact

Take a look at the *nosotros* and *vosotros* forms of *calentar*. As you can see, they are the only two forms that do not undergo a base change. As you'll notice with most irregular Spanish verbs, these two forms rarely undergo a base change.

The group of verbs that act similarly to *calentar* is not small. Refer to the following table for the infinitives and a sample conjugation (in the *yo* form, to show which vowel undergoes the change, and the *nosotros* form, where the root doesn't change).

▼ LIST OF VERBS WITH BASE CHANGE FROM *E* TO *IE*

Verb	Yo Form	Nosotros Form	English
advertir	*advierto*	*advertimos*	to warn
apretar	*aprieto*	*apretamos*	to tighten
arrendar	*arriendo*	*arrendamos*	to rent, to lease
ascender	*asciendo*	*ascendemos*	to ascend
cerrar	*cierro*	*cerramos*	to close
comenzar	*comienzo*	*comenzamos*	to begin

Verb	Yo Form	Nosotros Form	English
confesar	confieso	confesamos	to confess
convertir	convierto	convertimos	to convert
defender	defiendo	defendemos	to defend
discernir	discierno	discernimos	to discern
empezar	empiezo	empezamos	to begin
encender	enciendo	encendemos	to light, to turn on
entender	entiendo	entendemos	to understand
enterrar	entierro	enterramos	to bury
extender	extiendo	extendemos	to extend
herir	hiero	herimos	to injure
hervir	hiervo	hervimos	to boil
mentir	miento	mentimos	to lie, to deceive
merendar	meriendo	merendamos	to snack
negar	niego	negamos	to deny, to refuse
pensar	pienso	pensamos	to think
perder	pierdo	perdemos	to lose
preferir	prefiero	preferimos	to prefer
quebrar	quiebro	quebramos	to break
querer	quiero	queremos	to want, to love
recomendar	recomiendo	recomendamos	to recommend
sentir	siento	sentimos	to feel

Keep in mind that group irregularities are often limited to specific tenses and persons. Many of the words above follow the regular conjugations in other tenses. For example: *Hoy meriendo en casa.* (I snack at home today.) But: *Ayer, merendé en un restaurante.* (Yesterday, I snacked at a restaurant.)

Diphthong Base Change from *O* to *UE*

Another common diphthong base change among *-ar* and *-er* verbs (though not *-ir* verbs) is when the base vowel *o* changes to *ue*. Just as with the previous group of verbs, the *nosotros* and *vosotros* forms retain the base as it appears in the infinitive form. The following table provides a sample conjugation for the verb *mostrar* (to show, to exhibit). Notice that only the base of this verb is irregular—the endings remain the same as for any regular *-ar* verb.

▼ DIPHTHONG BASE CHANGE FROM O TO *UE*

	–ar	*mostrar* (to show, to exhibit)
yo	–o	*muestro*
tú	–as	*muestras*
él, ella, usted	–a	*muestra*
nosotros, nosotras	–amos	*mostramos*
vosotros, vosotras	–áis	*mostráis*
ellos, ellas, ustedes	–an	*muestran*

The following table lists common verbs that belong to the same group as *mostrar* and behave in a similar way.

▼ LIST OF VERBS WITH BASE CHANGE FROM O TO *UE*

Verb	Yo Form	Nosotros Form	English
absolver	*absuelvo*	*absolvemos*	to absolve
almorzar	*almuerzo*	*almorzamos*	to eat lunch
apostar	*apuesto*	*apostamos*	to bet
avergonzar	*avergüenzo*	*avergonzamos*	to embarrass
colgar	*cuelgo*	*colgamos*	to hang, suspend
comprobar	*compruebo*	*comprobamos*	to verify, to check
demostrar	*demuestro*	*demostramos*	to demonstrate
devolver	*devuelvo*	*devolvemos*	to return
encontrar	*encuentro*	*encontramos*	to find, to encounter
moler	*muelo*	*molemos*	to grind
morder	*muerdo*	*mordemos*	to bite
mover	*muevo*	*movemos*	to move
poder	*puedo*	*podemos*	to be able to
remover	*remuevo*	*removemos*	to remove, to dig
rogar	*ruego*	*rogamos*	to beg
soltar	*suelto*	*soltamos*	to release, to let go
soñar	*sueño*	*soñamos*	to dream
volar	*vuelo*	*volamos*	to fly
volver	*vuelvo*	*volvemos*	to return

Alert

There is a special case to the "*o* to *ue* group" irregularity. Fortunately, it is limited to one verb, *oler* (to smell). In addition to transforming the *o* to *ue*, as in other cases, there is an additional *h* added to the beginning of the word: *yo huelo, tú hueles, él huele, nosotros olemos, vosotros oléis, ellos huelen.*

Base Change from *E* to *I*

Another group of verbs, exclusively from the *–ir* category, undergoes a base change where the letter *e* changes to *i*. Once again, the *nosotros* and *vosotros* forms are the only ones not subject to this change. An example of this group is the verb *repetir* (to repeat)—see the following table on how it is conjugated.

▼ **DIPHTHONG BASE CHANGE FROM *E* TO *I* IN *–IR* VERBS**

	–ir	*repetir* (to repeat)
yo	*–o*	*repito*
tú	*–es*	*repites*
él, ella, usted	*–e*	*repite*
nosotros, nosotras	*–imos*	*repetimos*
vosotros, vosotras	*–ís*	*repetís*
ellos, ellas, ustedes	*–en*	*repiten*

The following table presents a list of verbs similar to *repetir* in their behavior in the present tense.

▼ **LIST OF VERBS WITH BASE CHANGE FROM *E* TO *I***

Verb	Yo Form	*Nosotros* Form	English
competir	*compito*	*competimos*	to compete
despedir	*despido*	*despedimos*	to see off, to fire
freír	*frío*	*freímos*	to fry
impedir	*impido*	*impedimos*	to impede
medir	*mido*	*medimos*	to measure

Verb	Yo Form	Nosotros Form	English
reír	río	reímos	to laugh
rendir	rindo	rendimos	to hand over
servir	sirvo	servimos	to serve
sonreír	sonrío	sonreímos	to smile
vestir	visto	vestimos	to dress

The following words also belong to the same group—in each one, the e changes to i. However, they are also irregular in other respects (described in the following sections of the chapter). For now, simply look at how they have been conjugated.

▼ BASE CHANGE FROM E TO I AND ADDITIONAL IRREGULARITIES

	–ir	conseguir (to obtain)	corregir (to correct)	elegir (to choose, to elect)	seguir (to follow)
yo	–o	consigo	corrijo	elijo	sigo
tú	–es	consigues	corriges	eliges	sigues
él, ella, usted	–e	consigue	corrige	elige	sigue
nosotros, nosotras	–imos	conseguimos	corregimos	elegimos	seguimos
vosotros, vosotras	–ís	conseguís	corregís	elegís	seguís
ellos, ellas, ustedes	–en	consiguen	corrigen	eligen	siguen

Spelling Accommodations

Think back to the verb corregir. You might have expected "I correct" to be translated as corrigo. Instead, in the irregular verb list earlier in this chapter, you saw it listed as corrijo. The j is used in place of the g so as to maintain the hard "hh" sound that is in the original word, corregir (coh-rreh-HHEER). Without this modification you would have had to pronounce it "coh-rreh-GHEER"—as you may remember, g is pronounced "hh" before e or i, and "gh" when it precedes any other letter.

The rule, then, is that when a verb ends with a *–ger* or *–gir*, the *g* changes to *j* whenever the verb ending does not end in an *e* or *i*—that is, the change only occurs in the *yo* form.

▼ **SPELLING ACCOMMODATION IN VERBS THAT END WITH –*GER* AND –*GIR***

	–er	*coger* (to grasp, to grab)	*–ir*	*finger* (to fake)
yo	*–o*	*cojo*	*–o*	*finjo*
tú	*–es*	*coges*	*–es*	*finges*
él, ella, usted	*–e*	*coge*	*–e*	*finge*
nosotros, nosotras	*–emos*	*cogemos*	*–imos*	*fingimos*
vosotros, vosotras	*–éis*	*cogéis*	*–ís*	*fingís*
ellos, ellas, ustedes	*–en*	*cogen*	*–en*	*fingen*

The following table presents other verbs that undergo a *g* to *j* change. Again, compare the *yo, nosotros,* and *ellos/ellas/ustedes* forms.

▼ –*GER* AND –*GIR* VERBS WITH SPELLING CHANGE FROM G TO J

Verb	Yo Form	Nosotros Form	Ellos/Ellas/ Ustedes Form	English
emerger	*emerjo*	*emergemos*	*emergen*	to emerge
escoger	*escojo*	*escogemos*	*escogen*	to choose
exigir	*exijo*	*exigimos*	*exigen*	to demand
proteger	*protejo*	*protegemos*	*protegen*	to protect
recoger	*recojo*	*recogemos*	*recogen*	to gather
restringir	*restrinjo*	*restringimos*	*restringen*	to restrict
surgir	*surjo*	*surgimos*	*surgen*	to surge, to appear

Verbs That End in –*GUIR*

In verbs that end in –*guir*, the *g* is pronounced as the "g" in "get"—the *u* is silent because it is there to keep the *g* hard (remember, –*gir* would sound like "hheer"). As you conjugate these verbs, you are trying to maintain a consistency of sound, which is why you need a modification in the *yo* form. Take a look at the following table.

▼ –*GUIR* VERBS THAT DROP THE *U* IN THE *YO* FORM

Verb	Yo Form	Nosotros Form	Ellos/Ellas/ Ustedes Form	English
conseguir	consigo	conseguimos	consiguen	to obtain
extinguir	extingo	extinguimos	extinguen	to extinguish
perseguir	persigo	perseguimos	persiguen	to pursue

As you can see, when you are conjugating verbs that end in –*guir*, you need to drop the *u* in the *yo* form. To do otherwise would be to change the hard *g* in –*guir* from "g" as in "get" to "gw" as in "Gwen." For example: *Consigo* would be *consiguo*, which would be pronounced "kohn-SEE-**gwoh**."

Other –*UIR* Verbs

This spelling accommodation focuses on other verbs that end in –*uir*. The modification is straightforward. The *i* is replaced by a *y* and the personal endings follow. The following table presents the conjugation of *huir* (to flee).

▼ SPELLING ACCOMMODATION IN OTHER –*UIR* VERBS

	–*ir*	*huir* (to flee)
yo	–o	huyo
tú	–es	huyes
él, ella, usted	–e	huye
nosotros, nosotras	–imos	huimos
vosotros, vosotras	–ís	huís
ellos, ellas, ustedes	–en	huyen

For the other verbs that behave like *huir* in the present tense, refer to the following table.

▼ OTHER –*UIR* VERBS THAT UNDERGO *I* TO *Y* CHANGE

Verb	Yo Form	Él/Ella/Usted Form	Nosotros	English
construir	construyo	construye	construimos	to construct
contribuir	contribuyo	contribuye	contribuimos	to contribute
destruir	destruyo	destruye	destruimos	to destroy

You may be wondering why the *i* needs to be replaced at all, and why it is kept in the *nosotros* form. Notice that in the infinitive and in the *nosotros* form, the weak vowels have only themselves to contend with. They share the same strength and are each given equal weight. You've seen before how a weak vowel reacts when it is adjacent to a strong one—the *i* tends to adopt a "y" sound and the *u* a "w" sound. In this case, the *u* must retain its own sound, and the only way to keep it independent is to convert the *i* to *y* and thus make the separation between *u* and a strong vowel clearer with a more explicit "y" sound.

Verbs That End with a Consonant and –*CER*

Verbs that end in –*cer* undergo spelling-accommodation changes in the *yo* form for the same reason that the –*guir* verbs undergo a change from *g* to *j*—in order to keep the pronunciation consistent. There are two changes that may occur.

 Fact

–*Cer* verbs must undergo a change in the *yo* form because if the –*er* is simply replaced by an *o*, the "s" sound produced by the *ce* combination in –*cer* would be transformed to a hard "k" sound.

The first scenario is that the base's final *c* may change to *z*. This occurs with verbs where the –*cer* ending is preceded by a consonant. For example, take the word *convencer* (cohn-behn-SEHR), meaning "to convince."

If you want to ascribe that action to yourself, you would say, "cohn-BEHN-soh," so it should be spelled *convenzo*. If you followed the regular-verb rule, you would have ended up with *convenco* (cohn-BEHN-coh) and, as a result, confuse a whole bunch of people. Refer to the following table for verbs that undergo this particular type of spelling accommodation.

▼ **SPELLING ACCOMMODATION FROM C TO Z**

	–er	convencer (to convince)	ejercer (to practice)	vencer (to conquer)
yo	–o	convenzo	ejerzo	venzo
tú	–es	convences	ejerces	vences
él, ella, usted	–e	convence	ejerce	vence
nosotros, nosotras	–emos	convencemos	ejercemos	vencemos
vosotros, vosotras	–éis	convencéis	ejercéis	vencéis
ellos, ellas, ustedes	–en	convencen	ejercen	vencen

 Alert

As you have already seen, a verb may undergo more than one change. In the first-person present-tense conjugation of *torcer* (to turn), for example, two changes occur: The *o* is replaced by *ue*, and the *–cer* changes to *–zo*: *tuerzo* (I turn), *tuerces* (you turn), *tuerce* (he, she, it turns; you turn), *torcemos* (we turn), *torcéis* (you turn), *tuercen* (they turn, you turn).

Verbs That End with a Vowel and –CER

If the letter that precedes the *–cer* ending in a verb is a vowel, the verb undergoes a slightly different transformation in the *yo* form of the present tense: In this case, the *–cer* ending changes to *–zco*. (This transformation is one of the many remnants left over from Latin.) The reasoning behind this transformation is similar—it is done to keep the *ce* sound that is voiced by the *z* in *–zco*.

▼ **EXAMPLE OF SPELLING ACCOMMODATION FROM *C* TO *ZC***

	–er	ofrecer (to offer)
yo	–o	ofrezco
tú	–es	ofreces
él, ella, usted	–e	ofrece
nosotros, nosotras	–emos	ofrecemos
vosotros, vosotras	–éis	ofrecéis
ellos, ellas, ustedes	–en	ofrecen

There are quite a few other verbs in Spanish that undergo this transformation in the *yo* form of the present tense.

▼ **VERBS WITH SPELLING ACCOMMODATION FROM *C* TO *ZC***

Verb	Yo Form	Él/Ella/Usted Form	English
agradecer	agradezco	agradece	to thank (for)
aparecer	aparezco	aparece	to appear
apetecer	apetezco	apetece	to desire, to crave
conocer	conozco	conoce	to be acquainted
crecer	crezco	crece	to grow
desaparecer	desaparezco	desaparece	to disappear
desobedecer	desobedezco	desobedece	to disobey
embellecer	embellezco	embellece	to embellish, beautify
empobrecer	empobrezco	empobrece	to impoverish
enriquecer	enriquezco	enriquece	to enrich
envejecer	envejezco	envejece	to grow old
establecer	establezco	establece	to establish
favorecer	favorezco	favorece	to favor
florecer	florezco	florece	to flower, to flourish
merecer	merezco	merece	to deserve
nacer	nazco	nace	to be born
obedecer	obedezco	obedece	to obey
padecer	padezco	padece	to suffer
parecer	parezco	parece	to seem

Of course, there are some exceptions to this general rule. Take a look at the verbs *hacer* (to do, to make), *cocer* (to cook), and *mecer* (to sway, to rock), conjugated in the following table. Their *yo*-form conjugations do not follow the rule established for verbs that end in –*cer* preceded by a vowel.

▼ EXCEPTIONS TO VERBS WITH SPELLING CHANGE FROM C TO ZC

	–er	*hacer* (to do, to make)	*cocer* (to cook)	*mecer* (to sway, to rock)
yo	–o	hago	cuezo	mezo
tú	–es	haces	cueces	meces
él, ella, usted	–e	hace	cuece	mece
nosotros	–emos	hacemos	cocemos	mecemos
ellos, ellas, ustedes	–en	hacen	cuecen	mecen

Verbs That End in –*UCIR*

Treat verbs that end in –*ucir* as verbs that end in –*cer* preceded by a vowel (see previous section). That is, the *c* is transformed to a *zc* in the *yo* form of these verbs following the same rule of spelling accommodation.

▼ EXAMPLE OF SPELLING ACCOMMODATION FROM C TO ZC

	–ir	*traducir* (to translate)	*cocer* (to cook)	*mecer* (to sway, to rock)
yo	–o	traduzco	cuezo	mezo
tú	–es	traduces	cueces	meces
él, ella, usted	–e	traduce	cuece	mece
nosotros, nosotras	–imos	traducimos	cocemos	mecemos
vosotros, vosotras	–ís	traducís	cuecen	mecen
ellos, ellas, ustedes	–en	traducen		

For a list of other –*ucir* verbs that behave similarly to *traducir*, refer to the following table.

▼ **VERBS WITH SPELLING ACCOMMODATION FROM C TO ZC**

Verb	Yo Form	Él/Ella/Usted Form	English
conducir	conduzco	conduce	to drive (a car)
deducir	deduzco	deduce	to deduce
introducir	introduzco	introduce	to introduce
lucir	luzco	luce	to shine
producir	produzco	produce	to produce

Adding Accent Marks to Weak Vowels

With Spanish verbs ending in –*uar*, some ending in –*iar*, and a few in –*ar*, the present-tense conjugations might sometimes require that the ordinarily weak vowels hold their own with the strong ones. In spelling, such vowels must be denoted with an accent mark. Look at what happens to *aislar* (to isolate), *enviar* (to send), and *actuar* (to act).

▼ **VERB CONJUGATIONS THAT REQUIRE ADDITIONAL ACCENT MARKS**

	–ar	aislar (to isolate)	enviar (to send)	actuar (to act)
yo	–o	aíslo	envío	actúo
tú	–as	aíslas	envías	actúas
él, ella, usted	–a	aísla	envía	actúa
nosotros, nosotras	–amos	aislamos	enviamos	actuamos
vosotros, vosotras	–áis	aisláis	enviáis	actuáis
ellos, ellas, ustedes	–an	aíslan	envían	actúan

Other examples of verbs that require accent marks in present-tense conjugations (except, of course, in the *nosotros* and *vosotros* forms) are listed in the following table.

▼ OTHER VERBS THAT REQUIRE ADDITIONAL ACCENT MARKS

Verb	Yo Form	Él/Ella/Usted Form	Nosotros Form	English
ahijar	ahíjo	ahíja	ahijamos	to adopt
aullar	aúllo	aúlla	aullamos	to howl, to shriek
continuar	continúo	continúa	continuamos	to continue

Unfortunately, this rule does not hold up for every *–iar* verb. The only way to know whether the *i* is accented is to memorize the exceptions. Look at the following table. Note that for each verb, the *i* is either accented in all the forms except *nosotros* and *vosotros,* or is not accented in any of the present-tense conjugations (except of course the accented *vosotros* ending *–áis*).

▼ ACCENT IRREGULARITIES IN –IAR VERBS

Verb	Yo Form (with *i*)	Verb	Yo Form (with *i*)
abreviar (to abbreviate)	abrevio	averiar (to damage)	averío
acariciar (to caress, to pet)	acaricio	confiar (to confide in)	confío
copiar (to copy)	copio	desviar (to deviate)	desvío
estudiar (to study)	estudio	guiar (to guide)	guío
rumiar (to ruminate)	rumio	vaciar (to empty)	vacío

Innate Irregularities

Recall that innate irregularities are those specific to verbs rather than groups of verbs. That is, the irregularities are not shared by different verbs across the three conjugations and are not simply spelling accommodations made to maintain consistent pronunciation.

Some verbs ending in *–er* or *–ir* may undergo a change in the *yo* form, where the ending becomes *–go*. This group may be divided into two subcategories: Some remain regular verbs in other forms, while others undergo base changes in second-, third-, or first-person plural forms.

Verbs that remain regular in all but the *yo* form are listed in the following table.

▼ **VERBS THAT END IN** *–GO* **IN THE** *YO* **FORM**

–ER/–IR Verb	Yo Form	*Él/Ella/Usted* Form	English
caer	caigo	cae	to fall
hacer	hago	hace	to do, to make
poner	pongo	pone	to put, to place
salir	salgo	sale	to leave, to go out

Other verbs, however, are irregular in more than one way. That is, in addition to the *–go* ending in the *yo* form, they undergo other irregularities in the base, such as an *i* to *ie* change (in *venir* and *tener*), an *i* to *y* change (see *oír*), or an *e* to *i* change (like in the verb *decir*). The following table provides these verbs' conjugations in the present tense.

▼ **VERBS WITH THE** *–GO* **TRANSFORMATION AND OTHER BASE IRREGULARITIES**

	venir (to come)	*tener* (to have)	*oír* (to hear)	*decir* (to say)
yo	vengo	tengo	oigo	digo
tú	vienes	tienes	oyes	dices
él, ella, usted	viene	tiene	oye	dice
nosotros, nosotras	venimos	tenemos	oímos	decimos
vosotros, vosotras	venís	tenéis	oís	decís
ellos, ellas, ustedes	vienen	tienen	oyen	dicen

Additional Irregular Verbs

Some irregular verbs do not seem to fit into any category. These verbs include *ir* (to go), *haber* (to have/be), and *caber* (to fit). You've already come across *ir* and *haber; caber* is conjugated in the following table. Please note that despite a radical change in the *yo* form, *caber* is actually regular in the other forms of the present tense.

▼ CONJUGATING *CABER* IN THE PRESENT TENSE

caber (to fit)	
yo	quepo
tú	cabes
él, ella, usted	cabe
nosotros, nosotras	cabemos
vosotros, vosotras	cabéis
ellos, ellas, ustedes	caben

CHAPTER 11

Direct and Indirect Objects

Y ou've learned about the subject of the sentence, and you've already covered quite a lot of ground on verbs. So what's next? Well, most of the time the subject and verb need an object, the target of the action done by the actor, so to speak. The following exercises will give you a solid overview of direct and indirect objects and object pronouns.

Transitive and Intransitive Verbs

Now that you've learned both the regular and irregular forms of the present-tense verbs, you might say that you can put together the most rudimentary sentences:

Salto.
I jump.

Devuelvas.
You return.

Competimos.
We compete.

These sentences describe simple actions. They are complete and self-contained. In some dictionaries, you will see their infinitives marked as *v.i. (verbo intransitivo).* Intransitive verbs are those verbs that can stand alone, without the need for further explanation.

But don't you feel like there is something missing? Some verbs may require an object—something that the verb acts upon. These verbs might be marked as *v.t. (verbo transitivo)*—transitive verb. For example, you can say, "I agree," which means "agree" is an intransitive verb. But you can't just say, "I need." Something is missing—you need *something*. That means "to need" is a transitive verb—it has to transition to an object, "a plan," "it," "something to eat," and so on.

Direct Objects

The word that a transitive verb needs to complete the phrase is known as the direct object. For examples of phrases with transitive verbs, as well as their corresponding direct objects, take a look at the following table.

▼ TRANSITIVE VERBS AND CORRESPONDING DIRECT OBJECTS

Transitive Verb Phrase	Direct Object	Question It Answers
I used to read . . .	newspapers.	(What did I used to read?)
I saw . . .	Roberto.	(Whom did I see?)
I drove . . .	a car.	(What did I drive?)
I should thank . . .	Marcos.	(Whom should I thank?)
I will search for . . .	the keys.	(What will I search for?)
I will search for . . .	María.	(Whom will I search for?)

The following are some examples of transitive verbs and direct objects in Spanish.

Leía dos periódicos cada día.
I used to read two newspapers every day.

Dejé mi coche en el garaje.
I left my car at the garage.

Agradezco a Marco sus atenciones.
I thank Marco for his attention.

Buscaré las llaves del coche.
I will search for the car keys.

Buscaré a María en su trabajo.
I will look for Maria at her job.

In these sentences, the newspapers, the car, the attention, the keys, and Maria all "act" as direct objects—objects that directly receive the actions of the sentences' verbs.

Direct-Object Pronouns

You have already learned about subject pronouns—pronouns that replace nouns to make the sentence shorter. For example, instead of saying "the girl from sixth grade, the one with short hair," you can simply say "she." Similarly, you can replace objects with object pronouns.

Let's say that you are talking about Maria. Maybe you searched for Maria at a party, or embraced Maria. In this example, "Maria" acts as a direct object. However, once you're talking about Maria, you can then switch to the direct-object pronoun, "her." The following table lists the direct-object pronouns available to you in Spanish.

▼ **DIRECT-OBJECT PRONOUNS**

Singular	Plural
me (me)	*nos* (us)
te (you, informal)	*os* (you, informal)
lo, la (you, formal)	*los, las* (you)
lo, la (him, her, it)	*los, las* (them)

This might seem a bit confusing to you. To make sense of all these pronouns, take a look at the following set of examples that illustrates the use of each direct-object pronoun.

Tú me ves.
You see me.

Hermanito, te veo ya.
Little brother, I already see you.

No lo encontré en el parque.
I didn't find him at the park.

La encontrarás mañana.
You will meet up with her tomorrow.

Señor, lo llevo a la calle Ochoa.
Sir, I'll take you to Ochoa Street.

Señora, la ayudo enseguida.
Madam, I'll help you in a second.

El profesor no nos alabó por el buen trabajo.
The professor did not praise us for the good work.

La agente os ayudará.
The agent will help you.

Carlos no los miró en el teatro.
Carlos did not see them at the theater.

Cuando vemos a las muchachas, las abrazamos.
When we see the girls, we hug them.

Las saludaré en la reunión.
I will greet you at the reunion.

María y Teresita, las buscaré por la tarde.
Maria and Teresita, I will look for you in the afternoon.

Are you beginning to see a pattern here? You probably noticed that in Spanish, the direct object is usually placed *before* and not *after* the verb. The following rules apply to using a direct object in Spanish:

- The direct-object pronoun is placed before the verb that is acting upon it as long as it is standing alone (you'll learn about the few exceptions later).
- The negation of a transitive verb requires that *no* be placed immediately before the direct object.
- Only transitive verbs require the use of a direct-object pronoun.

To Clarify the Direct-Object Pronoun

Along with the direct object, a Spanish speaker may add an additional phrase to help clarify the meaning of the direct object. For instance, in the phrase *las buscaré,* you might not always know based on the context whether *las* refers to "you" (feminine, formal) or "them" (feminine). To clarify, you might say *las buscaré a ellas* (I'll look for them) or *las buscaré a ustedes* (I'll look for you). *Las* and *a ellas* refer to the same thing—the object "them." The following table provides the relevant clarifying phrase for each object pronoun.

▼ OBJECT PRONOUNS AND PRONOUN PHRASES

Direct Object	English	Matching Pronoun Phrase
me	me	*a mí*
te	you (informal, singular)	*a ti*
lo	him, it, you (formal, singular)	*a él, a usted*
la	her, it, you (formal, singular, feminine)	*a ella, a usted*
nos	us	*a nosotros, a nosotras*
os	you (informal, plural)	*a vosotros, a vosotras*
los	them, you (formal, plural)	*a ellos, a ustedes*
las	them (feminine), you (formal, plural, feminine)	*a ellas, a ustedes*

For examples of how to use these direct-object phrases to emphasize or clarify who is being acted upon, take a look at the following group of phrases:

Me ven (a mí) bronceado.
They see me tanned./They see that I'm tanned.

Te llamaré (a ti) la semana próxima.
I will call you next week.

No lo encontré (a él) en el parque.
I didn't find him at the park.

No la encontré (a ella) en la casa.
I didn't find her at home.

La entiendo completamente (a usted).
I understand you completely.

Nos alabé (a nosotros) por el buen trabajo.
I praised us for the good work.

Os saludaré (a vosotros) cuando os encontraré.
I will greet you when I find you.

Las conocimos (a ellas) en la fiesta.
We got to know them at the party.

Reviewing the Personal A

As you already know, *a* may be translated as "to" and is sometimes used as a preposition of direction. For example:

¿Adónde van?
Where are you all going?

Vamos a la playa.
We are going to the beach.

However, when discussing it with respect to persons as direct objects, *a* doesn't really have a translation. It is used for nothing more than to indicate which person is the direct object. Take a look at how this plays out with the verb *mirar* (to look at, to watch):

Miro a mi esposa, a mi hija, y a mi hijo.
I look at my wife, daughter, and son.

Miro la cartelera encima del edificio.
I look at the billboard on top of the building.

See? No personal *a* is needed for the inanimate object, *la cartelera.* Here are a few more examples:

Esperaba el bus.
I was waiting for the bus.

Esperaba a Beti.
I was waiting for Betty.

Visité el museo.
I visited the museum.

Visité a mi mamá.
I visited my mom.

Escucho la música.
I listen to the music.

Escucho al sacerdote.
I listen to the priest.

There are some exceptions to keep in mind for the use of the personal *a*:

- Animals may take a personal *a* if they have some emotional tie or relationship to the speaker. For example: *Amo a mi perrito.* (I love my dear/little dog.) But: *Vi un perro.* (I saw a dog.)
- Direct objects used with *ser*, *tener*, and *haber* are not preceded by *a*. For example: *Soy Rodolfo* (I am Rodolfo). *Tengo tres primas.* (I have three cousins.)
- Only "concrete" personal direct objects are preceded by *a*; object abstracts of persons are not. For example: *Busco un hombre inteligente, fiel, y muy divertido.* (I am looking for an intelligent, faithful, and very funny man.)

Indirect Objects

Just as there are nouns or pronouns that directly interact with and complete the action of the verb, there are those that are related to the verb indirectly—they receive the completed action. These receivers are called indirect objects.

Indirect objects represent the nouns and pronouns that answer the questions "to whom" and "for whom" the verb's actions are intended. Take a look at the following sentences and try to figure out which are the direct objects and which are the indirect objects:

- I bought Laura a beverage.
- I will send you a letter.
- I brought my friends lunch.
- I recommend them movies.

The direct objects in the previous examples are "beverage," "letter," "lunch," and "movies." The indirect objects are "Laura," "you," "my friends," and "them." If you had trouble with these sentences, try reworking them so that the indirect objects are set apart:

- I bought a beverage for Laura.
- I will send a letter to you.
- I brought lunch for my friends.
- I recommend movies to them.

Indirect-Object Pronouns

The indirect-object pronouns in Spanish are very similar to the direct objects. In fact, the only point of confusion may be the third-person object pronouns. Take a look at the following tables, which contain pronouns for direct and indirect objects, and compare them.

▼ DIRECT-OBJECT PRONOUNS

Singular	Plural
me (me)	*nos* (us)
te (you, informal)	*os* (you, informal)
lo, la (you, formal)	*los, las* (you)
lo, la (him, her, it)	*los, las* (them)

▼ INDIRECT-OBJECT PRONOUNS

Singular	Plural
me (to me)	*nos* (to us)
te (to you, informal)	*os* (to you, informal)
le (you, formal)	*les* (you, formal)
le (to him, her, it)	*les* (to them)

 Alert

Use *le* and *les* for all indirect objects in the third person. *Le* should be used as any indirect-object pronoun in the singular: to him, her, it, or the formal you (*usted*). *Les* should be used as any indirect-object pronoun in the plural: to them (whether masculine or feminine), or to you, formal/plural (whether masculine or feminine as well).

The following examples will help you see how the indirect-object pronouns should be used in a Spanish sentence.

Él me compró una bicicleta.
He bought me a bicycle.

Te compré una bicicleta.
I bought you (informal/singular) a bicycle.

Le compré una bicicleta.
I bought you (formal/singular)/him/her a bicycle.

Ella nos compró una bicicleta.
She bought us a bicycle.

Ella os compró una bicicleta.
She bought you (informal/plural) a bicycle.

Les compré una bicicleta.
I bought you (formal/plural)/them a bicycle.

To review, here are some points to keep in mind about indirect-object pronouns:

- Indirect-object pronouns refer only to people.
- Indirect-object pronouns are almost always placed before the conjugated verb (exceptions will be covered later in this book).
- When *no* is necessary, place it before the indirect object. For example: *No me compró una bicicleta.* (He did not buy me a bicycle.)
- When *me*, *te*, or *nos* are used within a sentence that also employs a direct-object pronoun, they are placed immediately before the direct-object pronoun. For example: *Me la compró.* (He bought it for me.)
- Much like with the direct-object pronouns, you can use a redundant construction to emphasize who is receiving the completed action. For example: *Me compró a mí una bicicleta.* (He bought me a bicycle.)

- When *le* or *les* is used within a sentence that also employs a direct-object pronoun, it is replaced by *se*, which is then placed immediately before the direct-object pronoun. For example: *Le compré la bicicleta.* (I bought her a bicycle.) *Se la compré.* (I bought it for her.)
- In situations where an infinitive follows an active verb, the indirect-object pronoun may be placed either before the active verb or attached to the end of the infinitive, as follows: *Necesitas mandarle el regalo. Le necesitas mandar el regalo.* (You need to send him/her a present.)

The following are some examples of dealing with direct and indirect objects and object pronouns.

Quiero escribir una carta a Susana.
I want to write a letter to Susana.

Le quiero escribir una carta.
I want to write her a letter.

Quiero escribirle una carta.
I want to write her a letter.

Le quiero escribir a ella una carta.
I want to write her a letter.

Quiero escribirle a ella una carta.
I want to write her a letter.

Se la quiero escribir.
I want to write it to her.

Se la quiero escribir a ella.
I want to write it to her.

CHAPTER 12

Family and Friends

In this chapter, you will learn grammatical concepts that will broaden your scope to help you discuss topics related to your family and friends—possessive adjectives and pronouns, the impersonal *ser* construction to help you express possession, and the Spanish diminutives.

Possessive Constructions

If you think about it, a part of your identity is dependent on the relationships that you have, the relationships to which you belong. And as you belong to a relationship, the relationship "belongs" to you.

Spanish, as you may remember, does not facilitate the use of contractions to show possession. When you speak of "belonging" *en español*, you often mean that something is part "of" or "from" something else. For example:

Soy hijo de César y Patricia.
I am the son of Cesar and Patricia.

The preposition *de* links "son" to parents, where the "son" is "of" the parents. Another way of expressing this relationship is:

César y Patricia son los padres de Álex.
Cesar and Patricia are the parents of Alex.

Possessive Adjectives

You will have to rely on the *de* construction quite often, particularly when speaking of parts of a whole. However, when it becomes redundant, you can always rely on possessive adjectives to do the job—it's quicker and easier. Refer to the list of possessive adjectives in the following table.

▼ **POSSESSIVE ADJECTIVES**

Possession of One Object	Possession of Multiple Objects	English
mi	*mis*	my
tu	*tus*	your (informal, singular)
su	*sus*	his, her, its, your (formal, singular)
nuestro	*nuestros*	our (masculine/mixed)
nuestra	*nuestras*	our (feminine)
vuestro	*vuestros*	your (informal, plural, masculine/ mixed)
vuestra	*vuestras*	your (informal, plural, feminine)
su	*sus*	their, your (formal, plural)

🅔❗ Alert

In English, the adjectives used to show possession depend more on the person who has the items than on the items owned (possessed). Thus, you can use "my" to express ownership of a single item as well as many: my book, my books. In Spanish, however, a possessive pronoun will change depending on the number of the noun that it modifies: *mi libro, mis libros.*

To see how possessive adjectives work in Spanish, take a look at the following sentences.

Tengo mi propia computadora.
I have my own computer.

Compré mis libros en la librería.
I purchased my books at the bookstore.

Soy tu mejor amigo.
I am your best friend.

¿Visitaste a tus padres?
Did you visit your parents?

Conducirá su coche.
He will drive his car.

No conozco a sus hermanos.
I don't know her brothers.

¿Dondé está su libro, Sra. Lopez?
Where is your book, Mrs. Lopez?

Necesito sus consejos, Sr. García.
I need your advice, Mr. Garcia.

Estoy entusiasmado con nuestro viaje.
I am excited about our trip.

Escribiré nuestros nombres, Alicia y Carolina, en el registro.
I will write our names, Alicia and Carolina, on the register.

Es cuestión de vuestro agradecimiento.
It's a question of your gratitude.

Aquí están vuestras tazas de café.
Here are your cups of coffee.

Contaré su historia, la historia de Manuel y Jacinta.
I'll tell their story, the story of Manuel and Jacinta.

¿Ustedes buscan sus coches?
Are you looking for your cars?

 Alert

Remember to use a possessive adjective in front of every possessed noun listed. For example: *Hablé con tu hermana y tu primo.* (I spoke with your sister and cousin.)

Don't worry about the potential for confusion when employing possessive adjectives *su* and *sus*—they are generally clear in context. After all, you switch to a possessive adjective only after you've established the subjects or "possessors" in question. After all, you'd never say "her shoes" before you've made it clear to the speaker that you are referring to "Jane's shoes."

Possessive Pronouns

In addition to adjectives, *español* employs pronouns to show possession—the difference is that the possessive pronouns replace rather than describe nouns. Quick example: My books are mine. "My" is a possessive adjective describing "books." "Mine" is a possessive pronoun that replaces "books."

Like possessive adjectives, possessive pronouns reflect the number of items possessed. However, they must also agree in gender. Note that it is the gender and number of the items possessed (*not* the gender and number of the subject or "owner") that determines the gender of the possessive pronoun. Refer to the following table for a comprehensive list of possessive pronouns.

▼ **POSSESSIVE PRONOUNS**

Possession of One Object	Possession of Multiple Objects	English
mío	*míos*	mine, masculine
mía	*mías*	mine, feminine
tuyo	*tuyos*	yours (of *tú*), masculine
tuya	*tuyas*	yours (of *tú*), feminine
suyo	*suyos*	his, masculine
suya	*suyas*	his, feminine
suyo	*suyos*	yours (of *usted*), masculine
suya	*suyas*	yours (of *usted*), feminine
nuestro	*nuestros*	ours, masculine
nuestra	*nuestras*	ours, feminine
vuestro	*vuestros*	yours (of *vosotros*), masculine
vuestra	*vuestras*	yours (of *vosotros*), feminine
suyo	*suyos*	theirs, masculine
suya	*suyas*	theirs, feminine
suyo	*suyos*	yours (of *ustedes*), masculine
suya	*suyas*	yours (of *ustedes*), feminine

Check out the following examples.

Es mi casa. Es mía.
It's my house. It's mine.

Son sus regalos. Son suyos.
They're your presents. They're yours (of *usted*).

Son los problemas del profesor. Son suyos.
They're the professor's problems. They're his.

Es mi colchón. Es mío.
It's my mattress. It's mine.

Es tu corbata. Es tuya.
It's your tie. It's yours.

Son mis ideas. Son mías.
They're my ideas. They're mine.

Es su cuento. Es suyo.
It's your story. It's yours (of *ustedes*).

Son vuestros libros. Son vuestros.
They're your books. They're yours.

Es nuestra bicicleta. Es nuestra.
It's our bicycle. It's ours.

Son tus zapatos. Son tuyos.
They're your shoes. They're yours.

Es vuestra imágen. Es vuestra.
It's your image. It's yours.

Son nuestros coches. Son nuestros.
They're our cars. They're ours.

The Verb *Ser* and Possession

You've already learned that *ser*, a rather versatile Spanish verb, may express "to be" in six particular ways—personal identity, relationships, profession, origin, personality, and character appearance. To these six, you can also add possession. To review the conjugations of the verb *ser*, refer to the following table.

▼ CONJUGATING *SER*

Subject	Present	Preterite	Imperfect	Present-Perfect	Future
(yo)	*soy*	*fui*	*era*	*he sido*	*seré*
(tú)	*eres*	*fuiste*	*eras*	*has sido*	*serás*
(él, ella, usted)	*es*	*fue*	*era*	*ha sido*	*será*

Subject	Present	Preterite	Imperfect	Present-Perfect	Future
(nosotros, nosotras)	*somos*	*fuimos*	*éramos*	*hemos sido*	*seremos*
(vosotros, vosotras)	*sois*	*fuisteis*	*erais*	*habéis sido*	*seréis*
(ellos, ellas, ustedes)	*son*	*fueron*	*eran*	*han sido*	*serán*

The third person of the verb *ser* allows for a possessive construction, as in the following two examples:

El coche es mío. Es mi coche.
The car is mine. It is my car.

La casa es mía. Es mi casa.
The house is mine. It is my house.

This construction works in all of the verb tenses:

Fue mi coche.
It was/used to be my car (but no longer).

Era mi coche.
It was my car (and may or may not be now).

Ha sido mi coche desde hace cuatro años.
It has been my car since four years ago.

Será mi coche.
It will be my car.

What if you were talking about more than one car? How can this construction be expressed for plural items? Well, you simply use the third-person plural form of *ser: son* (in the present tense), and so on. Take a look at the following examples:

Son mis metas ahora.
They are my goals now.

Son mis metas cada vez que intento.
They are my goals each time I try.

Fueron mis metas.
They were/used to be my goals (but no longer).

Eran mis metas.
They were my goals.

Han sido mis metas desde la universidad.
They have been my goals since college.

Serán mis metas de hoy en adelante.
They will be my goals from now on.

The Family Gathering

In this section, you will practice expressing familial relationships. Take a look at the following table, which contains some relevant vocabulary.

▼ **VOCABULARY: FAMILIAL RELATIONSHIPS**

el abuelo, la abuela	grandparent; grandfather, grandmother
el ahijado, la ahijada	godchild; godson, goddaughter
el cuñado, la cuñada	brother-in-law, sister-in-law
el esposo, la esposa	spouse; husband, wife (Spain and Latin America)
el hermanastro, la hermanastra	stepbrother, stepsister
el hermano, la hermana	sibling; brother, sister
el hijastro, la hijastra	stepchild; stepson, stepdaughter
el hijo, la hija	child; son, daughter
la madrastra	stepmother

la madre, la mamá (mami)	mother, mom
el marido	husband (Spain)
la mujer	wife (Spain), woman, female
el nieto, la nieta	grandchild; grandson, granddaughter
el niño, la niña	child; boy, girl
la nuera	daughter-in-law
el padrastro	stepfather
el padre, el papá (papi)	father, dad
el primo, la prima	cousin
el sobrino, la sobrina	nephew, niece
el suegro, la suegra	father-in-law, mother-in-law
el varón	male, man
el yerno	son-in-law

Tips and Tricks

In general, there are a few things to remember when speaking of family relationships:

- When talking in general terms, or grouping family members by relationship rather than gender, you will often use the plural of the masculine form of the word. For example: *¿Cuántos hijos tienen Luis y Fanny?* (How many children do Luis and Fanny have?) *¿Quiénes son los padres de Hugo?* (Who are the parents of Hugo?)
- When grouping family members by relationship and gender, you will need to use the plural form of the word in the chosen gender. For example: *¿Cuántas sobrinas tiene César?* (How many nieces does Cesar have?)
- Since the masculine form is often used as the default gender of most categories, sometimes it may be necessary to further specify the male gender. For example: *¿Quiénes son los hijos (varones) de Luis y Fanny?* (Who are the sons of Luis and Fanny?)

Diminutives

When you hear a family member addressed in Spanish, you may not hear the standard relation terms you just saw above. In fact, you are more likely to hear variations on those terms. This is true because Spanish allows diminutive suffixes to be added to the ends of nouns. These suffixes are there to signal how the speaker feels about the person (or object) being described.

You will often encounter the *–ito* and *–ita* suffixes attached to masculine and feminine nouns and some adjectives. In general, they add a quality of "smallness" or "dearness" to the description of a noun.

 **Essential**

Although you are probably not aware of it, diminutives also occur in English. For example, compare the following: kitten/kitty, duck/ducky, dog/doggy. The difference is in terms of ease and frequency of usage: In Spanish, any noun can be easily changed to a diminutive by adding the appropriate suffix, and diminutives are used a lot more frequently.

Rules to Follow

When you wish to add a diminutive suffix, you need to keep a few things in mind. In general, nouns that end in vowels have the vowel replaced by the suffix appropriate in gender and number:

▼ **DIMINUTIVES**

la casa (the house)	*la casita* (the little house)
las cucharas (the spoon)	*las cucharitas* (the teaspoons)
el gato (the cat)	*el gatito* (the kitten)
la hermana (the sister)	*la hermanita* (the little/younger sister)
la lámpara (the lamp)	*la lamparita* (the little lamp)
los perros (the dogs)	*los perritos* (the puppies)

As with irregular verbs that require spelling accommodations, some diminutives also require certain modifications to maintain the pronunciation of the transformed nouns. Fortunately, the changes are similar to those you have already encountered.

Recall that if you wish a word to maintain a hard "c" sound, it must be replaced with a *qu* combination when adding a suffix that begins with *e* or *i: taco* (taco); *taquito* (little taco). Similarly, *g* is replaced by *gu: jugo* (juice), *juguito* (a little juice). *Z* sometimes needs to be replaced by *c: pedazo* (piece), *pedacito* (little piece).

If the noun ends in an *n* or *r*, add a *c* before the suffix: *joven* (youth), *jovencito* (young boy); *mujer* (woman), *mujercita* (young girl, woman).

If a noun with more than one syllable ends in *e*, you would also need to add a *c* before the suffix: *mueble* (furniture), *mueblecito* (small piece of furniture). If the first syllable of a two-syllable noun has an *ie* or an *ue*, and the last syllable ends in an *o* or an *a*, add the combination *ec* before the suffix: *cuento* (story), *cuentecito* (short story); *pierna* (leg), *piernecita* (small leg).

Appropriate Use

With respect to proper nouns and relationships, diminutives denote a particular closeness or affection for an individual. Most often, diminutives are used as forms of address. Given the affection that the diminutive implies, not using it may characterize a distance or formality within a relationship.

Keep in mind that diminutives are largely regional and the uses of *–ito* and *–ita* may differ from one country to the next. Other diminutives employed in addition to or instead of these suffixes include:

–ico/–ica: mata (bush), matica (little bush)

–illo/–illa: pan (bread), panecillo (bread roll)

Diminutives may also be employed with a limited number of adjectives. However, whereas diminutive nouns show a small size or affection, adding a diminutive suffix to an adjective will generally make its meaning more emphatic. For example: *suave* (soft), *suavecito* (very soft); *viejo* (old), *viejito* (a warm way of calling someone "old").

CHAPTER 13

Irregular Verbs: Moving Through Time

Irregular verbs in the present tense undergo various kinds of changes based on spelling modifications, group irregularities, and "innate" irregularities specific to a particular verb. The following sections will introduce you to how irregular verbs behave in the preterite, imperfect, present perfect, and future.

Conjugating the Preterite Tense

To review, the preterite tense deals with actions that occur in the past and have been completed. For regular-verb conjugations in the preterite, refer to the following table, which conjugates the regular verbs *cantar* (to sing), *aprender* (to learn), and *vivir* (to live).

▼ VERB CONJUGATIONS IN THE PRETERITE TENSE

–AR Verbs	*–ER* and *–IR* Verbs	
yo	*–é (canté)*	*–í (aprendí, viví)*
tú	*–aste (cantaste)*	*–iste (aprendiste, viviste)*
él, ella, usted	*–ó (cantó)*	*–ió (aprendió, vivió)*
nosotros, nosotras	*–amos (cantamos)*	*–imos (aprendimos, vivimos)*
vosotros, vosotras	*–asteis (cantasteis)*	*–isteis (aprendisteis, vivisteis)*
ellos, ellas, ustedes	*–aron (cantaron)*	*–ieron (aprendieron, vivieron)*

Spelling Accommodations

Whenever a particular conjugation ending threatens to change its pronunciation, the spelling of the verb must be altered to accommodate the correct pronunciation.

–AR Verb Irregularities

The first type of spelling accommodation that you might consider is in the verbs that end in –car. Because the yo ending is é, you need to find some way to accommodate the conjugation so that it keeps the "k" sound in –car. (You have already come across similar spelling-accommodation changes when learning about the irregular verbs in the present.) For example, take a look at the preterite conjugations of the verb buscar.

▼ CONJUGATING *BUSCAR* IN THE PRETERITE

	–ar	buscar (to search, to look for)
yo	–é	busqué
tú	–aste	buscaste
él, ella, usted	–ó	buscó
nosotros, nosotras	–amos	buscamos
vosotros, vosotras	–asteis	buscasteis
ellos, ellas, ustedes	–aron	buscaron

As you can see, in order to get a conjugation that is pronounced "boos-KEH," the c is changed to qu, which spells out busqué. For other verbs in this category, refer to the following table.

▼ OTHER –*CAR* VERBS

Verb	Yo Form	Él/Ella/Usted Form	English
abarcar	abarqué	abarcó	to take on
clarificar	clarifiqué	clarificó	to clarify
explicar	expliqué	explicó	to explain
practicar	practiqué	practicó	to practice
sacar	saqué	sacó	to take out
tocar	toqué	tocó	to touch, to play (an instrument)

Another spelling accommodation that occurs in the *yo* form of the preterite conjugation applies to verbs that end in *–gar*. In order to avoid the ending *–gé* (which makes the *g* soft), the spelling is modified to *–gué*.

Because only the *yo*-form ending of these verbs begins with an *e* (the only other vowel that would similarly influence *g* is *i*), only one out of the five conjugations is irregular. The following table lists most of the *–gar* verbs, as well as their conjugations in the *yo* form and the *él/ella/usted* form (used as an example of the "default" conjugation).

▼ *–GAR* VERB CONJUGATIONS

Verb	Yo Form	*Él/Ella/ Usted* Form	English
apagar	*apagué*	*apagó*	to turn off, to put out
entregar	*entregué*	*entregó*	to bring, to hand over
jugar	*jugué*	*jugó*	to play
llegar	*llegué*	*llegó*	to arrive
madrugar	*madrugué*	*madrugó*	to rise early
pagar	*pagué*	*pagó*	to pay
tragar	*tragué*	*tragó*	to swallow

The last exceptions for the first-person singular conjugations in the preterite that apply to *–ar* verbs are the verbs that end in *–zar*. When *–é* is added to the base, *z* must be replaced by *c*. This change may seem a bit confusing, since in most of the Spanish dialects both letters represent the same sound. Unfortunately, this is but another remnant of Spanish's heritage, when *z* and *c* had different pronunciations. Again, this spelling accommodation occurs only in the *yo* form of the preterite. For a list of *–zar* verbs, refer to the following table.

▼ *–ZAR* VERB CONJUGATIONS

Verb	Yo Form	*Él/Ella/Usted* Form	English
abrazar	*abracé*	*abrazó*	to embrace, to hug
almorzar	*almorcé*	*almorzó*	to eat lunch
empezar	*empecé*	*empezó*	to begin
rezar	*recé*	*rezó*	to pray

Base Ending in a Vowel

Look for *–er* and *–ir* verbs that have a base ending in a vowel; for example, *construir* (to construct)—its base ends in the vowel *u*. In this category, the *i* in third-person endings *–ió* and *–ieron* changes to a *y*. This switch does not indicate a fundamental change so much as it provides a clarification of emphasis. Remember that the *i* is a weak vowel that is often overpowered by stronger vowels (*a, e,* and *o*) to produce a "y" sound. Recall also that the accented *í* maintains its "ee" sound. An accented *í* would actually change the pronunciation of the word, and yet the "vowel + *i* + strong vowel" combination does not seem to produce a strong enough "y" to tame that mess of open sound. The answer therefore is to adopt the *y* formally. Refer to the conjugations of *construir* (to construct) and *sustituir* (to substitute) in the following table.

▼ CONJUGATING *CONSTRUIR* AND *SUSTITUIR* IN THE PRETERITE

	–uir	*construir* (to construct)	*sustituir* (to substitute)
yo	*–í*	*construí*	*sustituí*
tú	*–iste*	*construiste*	*sustituiste*
él, ella, usted	*–ió*	*construyó*	*sustituyó*
nosotros, nosotras	*–imos*	*construimos*	*sustituimos*
vosotros, vosotras	*–isteis*	*construisteis*	*sustituisteis*
ellos, ellas, ustedes	*–ieron*	*construyeron*	*sustituyeron*

In some of the verbs that belong to the same category (verb base ending in a vowel), there's an additional change: *Tú, nosotros,* and *vosotros* forms also have an accent mark over the *i*—the accent mark turns the weak *i* ("y") into a strong *í* ("ee"). For a sample conjugation, take a look at *proveer (to provide)*.

▼ **CONJUGATING *PROVEER* IN THE PRETERITE**

	−er	*proveer* (to provide)
yo	−*í*	*proveí*
tú	−*iste*	*proveíste*
él, ella, usted	−*ió*	*proveyó*
nosotros, nosotras	−*imos*	*proveímos*
vosotros, vosotras	−*isteis*	*proveísteis*
ellos, ellas, ustedes	−*ieron*	proveyeron

▼ **OTHER VERBS IN THE *I*-TO-*Y* CATEGORY**

Verb	Tú Form	Él/Ella/ Usted Form	Nosotros Form	Ellos/Ellas/ Ustedes Form	English
caer	*caíste*	*cayó*	*caímos*	*cayeron*	to fall
creer	*creíste*	*creyó*	*creímos*	*creyeron*	to believe
leer	*leíste*	*leyó*	*leímos*	*leyeron*	to read

Verbs That End in *−DUCIR*

In the case of verbs that end with *−ducir,* the irregular changes occur in *all* of the conjugations of the preterite tense. For example, take a look at how to conjugate *conducir* (to drive).

▼ **CONJUGATING *CONDUCIR* IN THE PRETERITE TENSE**

	conducir (to drive)
yo	*conduje*
tú	*condujiste*
él, ella, usted	*condujo*
nosotros, nosotras	*condujimos*
vosotros, vosotras	*condujisteis*
ellos, ellas, ustedes	*condujeron*

As you can see, three major changes have taken place: The *c* at the end of each base has been changed to *j*, the accent marks that generally appear in some of the preterite forms have all been dropped, and the ending in the third-person plural is –*eron* (not –*ieron*, as in regular –*er* and –*ir* verbs).

Other verbs that belong to this category appear in the following table.

▼ **SAMPLE –*DUCIR* VERB CONJUGATIONS IN THE PRETERITE**

Verb	Yo Form	Él/Ella/Usted Form	Ellos/Ellas/Ustedes Form	English
deducir	deduje	dedujo	dedujeron	to deduce
introducir	introduje	introdujo	introdujeron	to introduce
producir	produje	produjo	produjeron	to produce
traducir	traduje	tradujo	tradujeron	to translate

Another verb that is similar to this group (though, technically, it doesn't belong here) is *decir* (to say). In the preterite, its base changes to *dij*–, and its endings are the same as that of the verbs in this category: –*e*, –*iste*, –*o*, –*imos*, –*isteis*, and –*eron* (notice that there are no accent marks over these endings).

Group Irregularities

In the preterite, verbs that follow group irregularities may have vowel or consonant base changes. Each group is described in the following sections.

–*IR* Verb with Base Change from *E* to *I*

A few group-based irregularities have to do with vowel modifications. Some of these may be familiar to you from the present-tense irregular verb conjugations. For example, the following group of –*ir* verbs undergoes a base-vowel change from *e* to *i* in the third-person singular and third-person plural forms of the preterite verb. (Compare the base of the *yo* and *nosotros* forms to the *él/ella/usted* and *ellos/ellas/ustedes* forms in the following table.)

▼ **LIST OF VERBS WITH BASE CHANGE FROM *E* TO *I***

Verb	Yo Form	*Él/Ella/Usted* Form	*Nosotros* Form	*Ellos/Ellas/Ustedes* Form	English
advertir	*advertí*	*advirtió*	*advertimos*	*advirtieron*	to warn
medir	*medí*	*midió*	*medimos*	*midieron*	to measure
mentir	*mentí*	*mintió*	*mentimos*	*mintieron*	to lie
pedir	*pedí*	*pidió*	*pedimos*	*pidieron*	to ask
preferir	*preferí*	*prefirió*	*preferimos*	*prefirieron*	to prefer
repetir	*repetí*	*repitió*	*repetimos*	*repitieron*	to repeat
seguir	*seguí*	*siguió*	*seguimos*	*siguieron*	to follow
sentir	*sentí*	*sintió*	*sentimos*	*sintieron*	to feel
servir	*serví*	*sirvió*	*servimos*	*sirvieron*	to serve

–IR Verbs with Base Change from *O* to *U*

Although the group of verbs that falls into this category in the present tense is quite large, there are only two verbs (*dormir* and *morir*) that undergo this change in the preterite. Much like with the *e*-to-*i* change, only the bases of the third-person singular and plural conjugations undergo the change. For the conjugations, see the following table.

▼ **CONJUGATING *DORMIR* AND *MORIR* IN THE PRETERITE**

	–ir	*dormir* (to sleep)	*morir* (to die)
yo	*–í*	*dormí*	*morí*
tú	*–iste*	*dormiste*	*moriste*
él, ella, usted	*–ió*	*durmió*	*murió*
nosotros, nosotras	*–imos*	*dormimos*	*morimos*
vosotros, vosotras	*–isteis*	*dormisteis*	*moristeis*
ellos, ellas, ustedes	*–ieron*	*durmieron*	*murieron*

–ER Verbs with Base Change from *A* or *O* to *U*

The following verbs undergo a base change with the substitution of a *u* (note that, in some cases, the consonant following the base vowel will change as well, and the endings are also irregular). The *u* base change applies to all preterite conjugations of each of these verbs.

	caber (to fit)	*poder* (to be able to)	*poner* (to put)	*saber* (to know, learn)
yo	cupe	pude	puse	supe
tú	cupiste	pudiste	pusiste	supiste
él, ella, usted	cupo	pudo	puso	supo
nosotros, nosotras	cupimos	pudimos	pusimos	supimos
vosotros, vosotras	cupisteis	pudisteis	pusisteis	supisteis
ellos, ellas, ustedes	cupieron	pudieron	pusieron	supieron

Verbs with Base Change from *A* or *E* to *I*

Another irregularity is the substitution of a base vocalized by an *i*. Again, the best approach for these verbs is to memorize the irregular base and how the endings vary from the regular rule. For the conjugations of *i*-based verbs, refer to the following table.

▼ VERBS WITH BASE-VOWEL CHANGE TO *I*

	dar (to give)	*hacer* (to do, to make)	*querer* (to want, to love)	*venir* (to come)
yo	di	hice	quise	vine
tú	diste	hiciste	quisiste	viniste
él, ella, usted	dio	hizo	quiso	vino
nosotros, nosotras	dimos	hicimos	quisimos	vinimos
vosotros, vosotras	disteis	hicisteis	quisisteis	vinisteis
ellos, ellas, ustedes	dieron	hicieron	quisieron	vinieron

 Question

> **What's the correct translation of the verb *querer*?**
> Though *querer* is generally translated as "to want," it can also mean
> "to love" and "to like" (as in wanting). For instance: *¿Quiere un té?*
> means "Would you (formal, singular) like some tea?" The expression
> *te quiero* translates to "I love you."

You may have noticed that the *hic–* base of the preterite form of *hacer*
did undergo an additional change in the third-person singular (*él/ella/
usted*) form, where the *c* changed to a *z* (to form *hizo*). This is actually
a spelling-accommodation change—think about what would happen if
you didn't substitute the *z* for the *c*. You are trying to say "EE-soh"; spelling this conjugation *hico* would force you to change the pronunciation to
"EE-koh."

–*AER* Verbs with Base-Consonant Change to *J*

Consonant-based irregularities are similar to vowel-based ones. They
require changes or additions to a letter (in this case a consonant) within
the base of the verb. Also note that these conjugations may undergo
additional irregularities. For example, the accent marks may be dropped
from the first-person singular and third-person singular conjugations. The
verbs in the following group gain a *j*.

▼ –*AER* VERBS WITH BASE-CONSONANT CHANGE TO *J*

	abstraer (to make abstract)	*atraer* (to attract)	*contraer* (to contract)	*distraer* (to distract)
yo	*abstraje*	*atraje*	*contraje*	*distraje*
tú	*abstrajiste*	*atrajiste*	*contrajiste*	*distrajiste*
él, ella, usted	*abstrajo*	*atrajo*	*contrajo*	*distrajo*
nosotros, nosotras	*abstrajimos*	*atrajimos*	*contrajimos*	*distrajimos*
vosotros, vosotras	*abstrajisteis*	*atrajisteis*	*contrajisteis*	*distrajisteis*
ellos, ellas, ustedes	*abstrajeron*	*atrajeron*	*contrajeron*	*distrajeron*

Mixed Irregularities

Mixed irregularities combine vowel-based and consonant-based irregularities in their verbs. You have already encountered some of these verbs—just think back to the *ser* and *estar* chapter. Do you remember how to conjugate *estar* in the preterite? The base of this verb changes to *estuv–*. Another verb that behaves the same way is *tener (tuv–)*. And there is another verb that belongs to this category: *andar* (to walk). To compare the preterite conjugations of *andar, estar,* and *tener,* refer to the following table.

▼ CONJUGATING *ANDAR*, *ESTAR*, AND *TENER* IN THE PRETERITE TENSE

	andar (to walk)	*estar* (to be)	*tener* (to have)
yo	anduve	estuve	tuve
tú	anduviste	estuviste	tuviste
él, ella, usted	anduvo	estuvo	tuvo
nosotros, nosotras	anduvimos	estuvimos	tuvimos
vosotros, vosotras	anduvisteis	estuvisteis	tuvisteis
ellos, ellas, ustedes	anduvieron	estuvieron	tuvieron

Oír (to hear) is another irregular verb that is hard to categorize (as you might remember from looking at its conjugations in the present tense). The following table lists the conjugations of *oír* in the preterite.

▼ CONJUGATING *OÍR* IN THE PRETERITE TENSE

	oír (to hear)
yo	oí
tú	oíste
él, ella, usted	oyó
nosotros, nosotras	oímos
vosotros, vosotras	oísteis
ellos, ellas, ustedes	oyeron

Irregularities in Other Verb Tenses

The bad news is, we still have a number of tenses to cover. But the good news is, the rest of them aren't nearly as filled with irregularities as the preterite. Take a break, and then move on to review irregulars in the imperfect, present-perfect, and future tenses.

Imperfect Tense

In the imperfect tense, the endings always remain the same, just as in the regular-verb conjugations. Refer to the following table for a review of regular conjugations in the imperfect tense.

▼ CONJUGATING –*AR* VERBS IN THE IMPERFECT TENSE

Pronoun	Ending	*Cantar* (To Sing)
yo	–aba	cantaba
tú	–abas	cantabas
él, ella, usted	–aba	cantaba
nosotros, nosotras	–ábamos	cantábamos
vosotros, vosotras	–abais	cantabais
ellos, ellas, ustedes	–aban	cantaban

▼ CONJUGATING –*ER* AND –*IR* VERBS IN THE IMPERFECT TENSE

Pronoun	Ending	*Aprender* (To Learn)	*Vivir* (To Live)
yo	–ía	aprendía	vivía
tú	–ías	aprendías	vivías
él, ella, usted	–ía	aprendía	vivía
nosotros	–íamos	aprendíamos	vivíamos
vosotros, vosotras	–íais	aprendíais	vivíais
ellos, ellas, ustedes	–ían	aprendían	vivían

The few irregularities that exist in the imperfect are limited to innate base changes. One such example is the verb *ver* (to see). In the imperfect, the base changes from *v*– to *ve*–, so that you have *veía* (I saw) instead of *vía* (which is wrong and, incidentally, means "way" or "path" in Spanish). Refer to the following table to see how *ver* is conjugated in the imperfect.

yo	veía
tú	veías
él, ella, usted	veía
nosotros, nosotras	veíamos
vosotros, vosotras	veíais
ellos, ellas, ustedes	veían

Present-Perfect Tense

As you may remember, the present perfect is a composite tense—that is, it's made up of two verb parts: *haber* conjugated in the present tense, plus a past participle. To review the present-tense conjugations of *haber*, see the following table of regular present-tense conjugations.

▼ CONJUGATING VERBS IN THE PRESENT-PERFECT TENSE

Pronoun	−AR Verb	−ER Verb	−IR Verb
yo	he cantado	he aprendido	he vivido
tú	has cantado	has aprendido	has vivido
él, ella, usted	ha cantado	ha aprendido	ha vivido
nosotros, nosotras	hemos cantado	hemos aprendido	hemos vivido
vosotros, vosotras	habéis cantado	habéis aprendido	habéis vivido
ellos, ellas, ustedes	han cantado	han aprendido	han vivido

It follows, then, that the irregularities in the present perfect are really the irregularities in the past participles. The following table contains a list of verbs that have irregular past participles.

▼ IRREGULAR PAST PARTICIPLES

Infinitive	Past Participle	English
abrir	abierto	to open
cubrir	cubierto	to cover
decir	dicho	to say

escribir	escrito	to write
hacer	hecho	to do, to make
poner	puesto	to put
resolver	resuelto	to resolve
romper	roto	to break
satisfacer	satisfecho	to satisfy
ver	visto	to see
volver	vuelto	to return

Future Tense

In the future tense, irregularities are limited to innately irregular verbs. As a result, the endings employed are the same as those used with regular verbs. But first off, let's review regular verb endings in the future tense—refer to the following table for the conjugations.

▼ CONJUGATING VERBS IN FUTURE TENSE

	Verb Ending	*Cantar* (To Sing)	*Aprender* (To Learn)	*Vivir* (To Live)
yo	–é	cantaré	aprenderé	viviré
tú	–ás	cantarás	aprenderás	vivirás
él, ella, usted	–á	cantará	aprenderá	vivirá
nosotros, nosotras	–emos	cantaremos	aprenderemos	viviremos
vosotros, vosotras	–éis	cantaréis	aprenderéis	viviréis
ellos, ellas, ustedes	–án	cantarán	aprenderán	vivirán

There is a group of verbs that gain a *d* in the base that is used to put together the future-tense conjugations. These verbs are *poner* (to put), *salir* (to leave), *tener* (to have), and *venir* (to come). Since they have regular endings, the following table includes only some of the future-tense conjugations of these verbs.

▼ VERBS THAT GAIN A *D* IN THE BASE OF FUTURE-TENSE CONJUGATIONS

Verb	Yo Form	Él/Ella/Usted Form	Nosotros/Nosotras Form
poner (to put)	*pondré*	*pondrá*	*pondremos*
salir (to leave)	*saldré*	*saldrá*	*saldremos*
tener (to have)	*tendré*	*tendrá*	*tendremos*
venir (to come)	*vendré*	*vendrá*	*vendremos*

Another group of verbs modifies its base by dropping an *e*. (A likely explanation might be that dropping this vowel shortened the pronunciation of these verbs by a syllable.) For a list of these verbs, refer to the following table.

▼ VERBS THAT LOSE AN *E* IN THE BASES OF FUTURE-TENSE CONJUGATIONS

Verb	Yo Form	Él/Ella/Usted Form	Nosotros/Nosotras Form
caber (to fit)	*cabré*	*cabrá*	*cabremos*
poder (to be able to)	*podré*	*podrá*	*podremos*
saber (to know)	*sabré*	*sabrá*	*sabremos*

Finally, there are some verbs that are just hard to classify. You've seen them come up again and again in the chapters on irregular verbs: *decir* (to say), *hacer* (to do, to make), and *querer* (to want, to love). Their conjugations are listed in the following table.

▼ OTHER VERBS WITH IRREGULAR FUTURE-TENSE CONJUGATIONS

Verb	Yo Form	Él/Ella/Usted Form	Nosotros Form
decir (to say)	*diré*	*dirá*	*diremos*
hacer (to do, to make)	*haré*	*hará*	*haremos*
querer (to want, to love)	*querré*	*querrá*	*querremos*

CHAPTER 14

Impersonal Assertions and the Subjunctive

You probably remember your old English teacher warning everybody about overusing passive-voice sentences like "it was given to me by Eileen" (instead of "Eileen gave it to me"). But sometimes you do need to use impersonal constructions, and you may also want to know how to do so in Spanish. Whereas we rarely use subjunctive mood in English, it's a far more useful concept in Spanish, and worth learning about.

Impersonal Assertions

Most passive-voice constructions in English come with the verb form of "to be." In Spanish, you will often use *ser* as the equivalent. One type of passive-voice construction that uses *ser* is the impersonal assertion. Impersonal assertions are those statements that are said as general truths. They are not bound to time—they may have been true before, may be true now, and might be true in the future. The general rule is that they are expressed in the third person of the present tense with the verb *ser*.

Recall that the interaction of the verb *ser* (to be) and the object of possession permitted you to say *es mi abrigo* (it's my coat). Following are some examples of impersonal-assertion sentences:

Es malo fumar.
It's bad to smoke.

Es bueno hacer ejercicios.
It's good to exercise.

Es inteligente tomar notas.
It's smart to take notes.

 **Essential**

The easiest way to distinguish impersonal constructions is to remember that they do not have a specific subject. Technically, of course, the subject is the pronoun of *ser* (*él* or *ella* for *es*, and *ellos* or *ellas* for *son*, translated into English as "it"), but it does not refer to anything and is never actually present in the meaning of the sentence.

Discussing the Weather

The impersonal construction may be used to discuss *el tiempo* (the weather). However, since the weather is never in a permanent state, the verb *estar* is used instead of *ser*.

Estar allows you to describe physical conditions; when employed to describe the environment, *estar* may be translated as "it is." Take a look at the following questions:

¿Cómo está el clima?
How is the climate?

¿Cómo está el tiempo?
How is the weather?

¿Cómo está afuera?
How is it outside?

In reply, all you need to do is say *Está* ... and a word that would describe the weather. For a list of weather-related vocabulary, check out the following table.

▼ **THE VOCABULARY OF WEATHER**

agradable	pleasant
buen tiempo	nice weather
caluroso	hot
claro	clear
cubierto	covered (with clouds)
despejado	without clouds
frío	cold
helado	freezing
húmedo	humid
lluvioso	rainy
nevado	snowy
nublado	cloudy
con mucho viento	windy

What's the Weather Doing?

You can also use *hacer* to describe what the weather "does" (as opposed to how it "is"). For instance, *hace sol* may be translated as "it's sunny," but this phrase literally stands for "(the weather) makes the sun."

So another way of asking about the weather is *¿Qué tiempo hace?* ("How is the weather?" or "Which weather is going on?"). In reply, you would say, *Hace . . .*

Hace buen tiempo.
The weather is nice.

Hace calor.
It's hot.

Hace frío.
It's cold.

Hace viento.
It's windy.

Other Weather-Related Verbs

In addition to *estar* and *hacer*, you can use other verbs that describe the weather. Take a look at the following table for some examples. Notice that most of these verbs look like the adverbs you've learned already to describe the weather.

▼ **VERBS TO USE IN DESCRIBING THE WEATHER**

amanecer	to grow light (at dawn)
anochecer	to grow dark (at night)
granizar	to hail
helar	to freeze
llover	to rain
lloviznar	to drizzle
relampaguear	to flash with lightning
tronar	to thunder

Imperative Constructions

Another type of construction that lacks a voiced subject is the imperative construction. The imperative is often called the command mood, though it's not used solely for commands but also in making requests. When you request, ask, or demand something addressing yourself directly to someone, you are using the imperative.

The imperative mood's concern with the present should make it a fairly easy mood to master. Simply plug in the appropriate endings and place the command within exclamation marks (¡ . . . !) for emphasis. Note that there are only *tú, usted, nosotros, vosotros,* and *ustedes* forms in the command mood, because you must address a "you" (*nosotros* form, to be explained in greater detail, is a "let's . . ." construction). However, the tricky thing is that endings vary depending on whether the command is positive (do!) or negative (don't!).

Tú in the Imperative

The best way to approach the imperative is by learning the *tú* form. That's because it's the most obvious type of command—you are much more likely to use the imperative with somebody you know well, or somebody who is younger than you.

▼ **POSITIVE COMMANDS ADDRESSED TO *TÚ***

−AR Verb	*−ER* Verb	*−IR* Verb
¡Camina! (Walk!)	*¡Bebe!* (Drink!)	*¡Recibe!* (Get!)

▼ **NEGATIVE COMMANDS ADDRESSED TO *TÚ***

−AR Verb	*−ER* Verb	*−IR* Verb
¡No camines! (Don't walk!)	*¡No bebas!* (Don't drink!)	*¡No recibas!* (Don't receive!)

It is understandable if you find these a little confusing. The positive command endings are the same for the imperative *tú* form as they are for the indicative present-tense *él/ella/usted* form: *camina, bebe, recibe*.

Whereas the positive imperatives for *tú* take the same form as the indicative present-tense conjugations of the more formal *usted*, negative imperatives of *tú* seem to invert the present-tense *tú* conjugation endings. *Caminar* takes on the *−es* ending, and *beber* and *recibir* take on the *−as* ending: *no camines, no bebas, no recibas*.

There are only a few verbs that have irregular positive-*tú* command conjugations—that is, verbs that don't simply follow the rules outlined here. These verbs are listed in the following table.

▼ **IRREGULAR VERBS**

Verb	English	Positive *Tú* Command	Negative *Tú* Command
decir	to say	*¡Di!*	*¡No digas!*
hacer	to do, to make	*¡Haz!*	*¡No hagas!*
ir	to go	*¡Ve!*	*¡No vayas!*
poner	to put	*¡Pon!*	*¡No pongas!*
salir	to leave	*¡Sal!*	*¡No salgas!*
ser	to be	*¡Sé!*	*¡No seas!*
tener	to have	*¡Ten!*	*¡No tengas!*
venir	to come	*¡Ven!*	*¡No vengas!*

Vosotros/Vosotras in the Imperative

There is also a *vosotros/vosotras* form for the imperative mood. To make a positive *vosotros* command, drop the final *r* of the verb's infinitive and replace it with a *d*: *caminad, bebed, recibid.*

The only exception to this rule is the verb *ir* (to go): the positive form in the command mood is *id*:

¡Id a casa ahora mismo!
Go home immediately!

To make negative *vosotros* commands, use the present-tense verb endings, but switch the endings of *–ar* and *–er/–ir* verbs, as you've done with the negative *tú* commands: *no caminéis, no bebáis, no recibáis.*

To review the *vosotros/vosotras* command conjugations, see the following table:

▼ **POSITIVE COMMANDS ADDRESSED TO *VOSOTROS/VOSOTRAS***

–AR Verb	–ER Verb	–IR Verb
¡Caminad! (Walk!)	*¡Bebed!* (Drink!)	*¡Recibid!* (Receive!)

▼ **NEGATIVE COMMANDS ADDRESSED TO *VOSOTROS/VOSOTRAS***

–AR Verb	–ER Verb	–IR Verb
¡No caminéis! (Don't walk!)	*¡No bebáis!* (Don't drink!)	*¡No recibáis!* (Don't receive!)

Usted/Ustedes and Nosotros/Nosotras in the Imperative

The commands or requests addressed to *usted, ustedes, nosotros,* and *nosotras* approach the imperative in the same way as the negative *tú/vosotros/vosotras* commands. That is, you add *–e, –en,* and *–emos* endings to the *–ar* verbs, and *–a, –an,* and *–amos* endings to the *–er* and *–ir* verbs. This rule applies to both positive and negative commands.

▼ **POSITIVE COMMANDS TO *USTED*, *USTEDES*, AND *NOSOTROS/NOSOTRAS***

Pronoun	−*AR* Verb	−*ER* Verb	−*IR* Verb
usted	¡Camine!	¡Beba!	¡Reciba!
ustedes	¡Caminen!	¡Beban!	¡Reciban!
nosotros, nosotras	¡Caminemos!	¡Bebamos!	¡Recibamos!

▼ **NEGATIVE COMMANDS TO *USTED*, *USTEDES*, AND *NOSOTROS/NOSOTRAS***

Pronoun	−*AR* Verb	−*ER* Verb	−*IR* Verb
usted	¡No camine!	¡No beba!	¡No reciba!
ustedes	¡No caminen!	¡No beban!	¡No reciban!
nosotros, nosotras	¡No caminemos!	¡No bebamos!	¡No recibamos!

 **Essential**

In the *nosotros/nosotras* form, the commands may be translated in the form of "let's . . ." This means ¡*Caminemos!* translates to "Let's walk!"; ¡*Bebamos!* is "Let's drink!"; and ¡*Recibamos!* may be translated as "Let's receive (something)!"

Irregular *Nosotros/Nosotras* Conjugations

Some verbs undergo a spelling accommodation in the *nosotros/nosotras* form of the imperative. Verbs that end in *−car*, *−gar*, and *−zar* follow a base consonant change from *c* to *qu*, *g* to *gu*, and *z* to *ce*, respectively. See the following tables for details.

▼ **CONSONANT CHANGE IN *−CAR* VERBS**

Verb	English	Imperative *Nosotros/Nosotras* Form
abarcar	to take on	abarquemos
buscar	to look for	busquemos
practicar	to practice	practiquemos
sacar	to take out	saquemos

▼ CONSONANT CHANGE IN –GAR VERBS

Verb	English	Imperative *Nosotros/Nosotras Form*
apagar	to turn off	apaguemos
entregar	to hand over	entreguemos
jugar	to play	juguemos
llegar	to arrive	lleguemos

▼ CONSONANT CHANGE IN –ZAR VERBS

Verb	English	Imperative *Nosotros/Nosotras* Form
abrazar	to embrace, to hug	abracemos
almorzar	to eat lunch	almorcemos
empezar	to begin	empecemos
rezar	to pray	recemos

Another group of irregular verbs belongs to the *–ir* category, and the spelling-accommodation changes involved concern the verb's base vowel. The changes usually occur as follows: from *e* to *i,* and from *o* to *u.* See the following two tables.

▼ VOWEL CHANGE FROM *E* TO *I*

Verb	English	Imperative *Nosotros/Nosotras Form*
advertir	to warn	advirtamos
medir	to measure	midamos
mentir	to lie, to deceive	mintamos
pedir	to ask, to request	pidamos

▼ VOWEL CHANGE FROM *O* TO *U*

Verb	English	Imperative *Nosotros/Nosotras Form*
dormir	to sleep	durmamos
morir	to die	muramos

Object Pronouns in Commands

Object pronouns generally precede the verb:

Lo vi en la calle.
I saw him on the street.

Lo hice a las nueve de la mañana.
I did it at nine in the morning.

In positive commands, the object pronoun is attached to the verb of command:

¡Estúdialo ahora mismo!
Study it right now!

¡Bébanlo después de comer!
Drink it after eating!

¡Abrámoslo mañana!
Let's open it tomorrow!

¡Escúchame!
Listen to me!

¡Dame la blusa!
Give me the blouse!

¡Dámela!
Give it to me!

In some cases, when you add additional syllables to a word, you also need to add an accent mark—unless you intend to pronounce it differently. For example, take a look at *¡Dame!* and *¡Dámela!* According to accent rules, a word that ends in a vowel should be accented on the next-to-last syllable. When you add *la,* you also need to add an accent mark over the *a* in order to keep the pronunciation "DAH-meh-lah" (and not "dah-MEH-lah"). Note that in the last example the indirect object *me* (to me) precedes the direct object *la* (it).

In the negative, however, the object pronoun precedes the imperative verb (though, once again, the indirect object comes first, followed by the direct object). Take a look at the following examples:

¡No me escuches!
Don't listen to me!

¡No me des la blusa!
Don't give me the blouse!

¡No me la des!
Don't give it to me!

Introducing the Subjunctive

As you saw earlier, an impersonal assertion tries to lend a certain amount of authority or objectivity to a statement. An easy way to create this impression is to use the phrases that lend themselves to its construction. Some of these phrases include:

Es evidente que . . .
It is evident that . . .

Es cierto que . . .
It is certain that . . .

Es verdad que . . .
It is true that . . .

Es seguro que . . .
It is sure that . . .

Es indudable que . . .
It is indubitable that . . .

Es que . . .
It is that . . .

To see how these constructions behave in complete sentences, look at the following examples:

Será feliz quien tiene a quien amar.
One who has someone to love will be happy.

Es indudable que los hijos necesitan a su madre.
There is no doubt that children need their mother.

Es seguro que el policía lo cogerá.
It's sure that the policeman will catch him.

All of these constructions express opinions of certainty in the indicative mood. As you've seen before, this mood can also express some uncertainty, particularly in the compound tenses using a form of *haber*. Recall, however, that usually the uncertainty that can be created is somewhat limited—a probability by definition implies that there is a chance that the contrary may occur, but the deck is stacked in favor of the outcome. The indicative offers the following sentence qualifiers:

A lo mejor voy de vacaciones a Perú.
I may go on vacation to Peru.

Quizás llega a tiempo el regalo de Navidad.
Hopefully the Christmas present arrives on time.

Tal vez no le gustan los camarones.
Perhaps she doesn't like shrimp.

Posiblemente el remedio es demasiado fuerte.
Possibly the remedy is too strong.

Though the ability to express uncertainty can be found in the indicative mood, the degree of doubt or opinion is very constrained. To more forcefully express the gray areas of life, you need to consider the subjunctive mood, which may be novel to you, given its scarce employment in everyday English.

Recall that the mood associated with verbs is the manner by which you decide to communicate or report the world around you. In the indicative, you were concerned with telling how things appeared—a somewhat "objective" accounting. In contrast, the subjunctive takes on a somewhat "subjective" approach. It allows you to express opinions, personal as well as impersonal.

In the present subjunctive, the conjugations are similar to the present indicative, except that they're inverted (you've already seen this in the imperative conjugations). Take a look at the following tables for details.

▼ CONJUGATING THE –AR VERB CANTAR (TO SING) IN THE PRESENT SUBJUNCTIVE

yo	–e	cante
tú	–es	cantes
él, ella, usted	–e	cante
nosotros, nosotras	–emos	cantemos
vosotros, vosotras	–éis	cantéis
ellos, ellas, ustedes	–en	canten

▼ CONJUGATING THE –ER VERB APRENDER (TO LEARN) IN THE PRESENT SUBJUNCTIVE

yo	–a	aprenda
tú	–as	aprendas
él, ella, usted	–a	aprenda
nosotros, nosotras	–amos	aprendamos
vosotros, vosotras	–áis	aprendáis
ellos, ellas, ustedes	–an	aprendan

▼ **CONJUGATING THE –IR VERB VIVIR (TO LIVE) IN THE PRESENT SUBJUNCTIVE**

yo	–a	viva
tú	–as	vivas
él, ella, usted	–a	viva
nosotros, nosotras	–amos	vivamos
vosotros, vosotras	–áis	viváis
ellos, ellas, ustedes	–an	vivan

As you can see, the –ar present-subjunctive endings are similar to the –er endings of the present indicative. Likewise, the present subjunctive –er and –ir endings are almost the same as those of the –ar present indicative. The one difference is that the yo and él/ella/usted forms are identical in the subjunctive.

So, now that you've got the conjugations down, the next step is to figure out when you need to switch to the subjunctive mood.

 Essential

A subjunctive phrase rarely stands alone. At the heart of most sentences that use the present subjunctive, there is an indicative phrase that sets the subjunctive in motion by introducing a need or desire to be met, a doubt to be expressed, or an opinion to be made. The short sentence is largely absent in the subjunctive.

Expressing Uncertainty

As you saw earlier, certain "keywords" may be employed to express doubt. Such keywords in the subjunctive include words like "maybe" and "possibly":

Quizás llegue a tiempo el regalo de Navidad.
Hopefully the Christmas present arrives on time (but there is a good chance that it won't).

Tal vez no le gusten camarones.
Perhaps she doesn't like shrimp (but she may).

Posiblemente el remedio sea demasiado fuerte.
Possibly the remedy is too strong (but it may be otherwise).

Although the sentences are very similar to the ones you've seen previously, the fact that you are using the subjunctive lends them a sense of uncertainty—hence the additional phrases included in parentheses in the translations. Other tags of uncertainty specifically useful in the subjunctive include "it's doubtful that" and "it might be that":

Es dudoso que Mario saque buena nota en la prueba.
It is doubtful that Mario gets a good grade on the test.

Es posible que lo llame por teléfono mañana.
It's possible that I might call him tomorrow.

Puede ser que compre un coche usado.
It might be that I'll purchase a used car.

Puede que el dueño cambie de idea.
It could be that the owner changes his mind.

Notice in the previous sentences how *que* introduces the subjunctive phrase, a common way of signaling the subjunctive. Often, the subjunctive is found as a dependent clause that relies on a main independent and indicative clause to exist.

The following are groups of verbs that take on a subjunctive *que* clause:

▼ **THE SUBJUNCTIVE *QUE* CLAUSE**

Doubt or Uncertainty	
dudar	to doubt
no estar seguro	not to be sure
imaginarse	to expect

Hope or Necessity	
esperar	to hope, to wait for
necesitar	to need
preferir	to prefer
querer	to want, to love
Emotional State	
alegrar	to make happy
enojar	to make angry
gustar	to like
sentir	to feel
sorprender	to surprise
Telling or Asking	
aconsejar	to advise
decir	to say
exigir	to demand
insistir	to insist
pedir	to ask
prohibir	to forbid
rogar	to beg

Here are some examples:

Dudamos que usted tenga suficiente valor.
We doubt that you have enough courage.

Ellos prefieren que nieve.
They prefer that it snow.

Me enoja que vosotros todavía no vayáis a la escuela.
It makes me angry that you still don't go to school.

Ojalá que el próximo año sea mejor.
Let's hope that next year is better.

Perfect Tenses in the Subjunctive

The subjunctive mood also has two perfect tenses: the present perfect and past perfect. These tenses are not used frequently and will only be given a brief introduction here.

The rules for using subjunctive in the perfect tenses are the same as in the present subjunctive for the most part. Like all perfect tenses, perfect subjunctives (past and present) pair *haber* with the past participle.

The present-perfect subjunctive is used when the main verbal clause is in the present tense. The following table lists the present-perfect conjugations of *haber.*

▼ **PRESENT-PERFECT CONJUGATIONS OF** *HABER*

yo	*haya*
tú	*hayas*
él, ella, usted	*haya*
nosotros, nosotras	*hayamos*
vosotros, vosotras	*hayáis*
ellos, ellas, ustedes	*hayan*

Here are some examples of how the present-perfect subjunctive may be used:

Quiero que hayan terminado el examen.
I want them to have finished the test.

Ella busca a una persona que haya visitado este museo.
She is looking for a person who has visited this museum.

The past-perfect subjunctive is the subjunctive equivalent of a perfect past tense, and it is often used when the main verbal clause of the sentence is in the preterite, imperfect, or conditional tense. First, let's look at the past-perfect subjunctive conjugations of *haber.* (Note that these are the imperfect subjunctive endings.)

▼ PAST-PERFECT SUBJUNCTIVE CONJUGATIONS OF *HABER*

yo	hubiera
tú	hubieras
él, ella, usted	hubiera
nosotros, nosotras	hubiéramos
vosotros, vosotras	hubierais
ellos, ellas, ustedes	hubieran

Here are some examples:

Era posible que ustedes no hubieran sabido la verdad.
It was possible that you hadn't known the truth.

Si yo me hubiera escondido, ellos no me habrían encontrado.
If I had hidden myself, they wouldn't have found me.

CHAPTER 15

What You Like to Do

What do you like to do in your "free" time? Of course, you probably have many *deberes* (obligations), but you also entertain yourself with things that you enjoy. This chapter will help you explore your hobbies and pastimes in Spanish.

Likes and Dislikes

The verb that will help you indicate your preferences is *gustar*. To translate, "I like hamburgers," use *gustar*, but switch the subject and object around, so that the subject is what pleases you (hamburgers) and the object is "I": *Me gustan las hamburguesas.* (Literally: "Hamburgers please me.")

Because the subject of these sentences is something that is liked, it can either be singular or plural, but it is always in third person, so you only have *gusta* and *gustan* as verb choices (assume you stay in the present tense). As for the object, it is always an indirect-object pronoun: me, you, him, her, it, us, them. Take a look at the following examples:

Me gusta el café.
I like coffee.

Me gustan las flores.
I like flowers.

Te gusta el café.
You like coffee.

Te gustan las flores.
You like flowers.

Le gusta el café.
He/she likes coffee. / You like coffee. (*usted*)

Le gustan las flores.
He/she likes flowers. / You like flowers. (*usted*)

Nos gusta el café.
We like coffee.

Nos gustan las flores.
We like flowers.

Os gusta el café.
You like coffee. (*vosotros*)

Os gustan las flores.
You like flowers. (*vosotros*)

Les gusta el café.
They like coffee. / You like coffee. (*ustedes*)

Les gustan las flores.
They like flowers. / You like flowers. (*ustedes*)

So what if what you like is not a thing, but an action? For example, how would you say "I like to travel"? Think of this phrase as "I like traveling." Since "traveling" may be thought of in the singular, you would say *Me gusta viajar.*

In Combination with *Gustar*

Keep in mind that as simple as this construction is to use, there are certain combinations of words that may change what you mean to say. For instance, be sure to put the modifier in the right place. Compare the following:

Me gusta mucho viajar.
I really like to travel.

Me gusta viajar mucho.
I like to travel a lot/often.

Untranslatable redundant constructions may also be used to emphasize or clarify the indirect object. Review the following examples:

A mí me gusta el boxeo.
El boxeo me gusta a mí.
I like boxing.

A ti te gusta la ópera.
La ópera te gusta a ti.
You like the opera.

A él le gusta María.
María le gusta a él.
He likes Maria.

A ella le gustan los perros.
Los perros le gustan a ella.
She likes dogs.

A usted le gusta la pesca.
La pesca le gusta a usted.
You like fishing.

A nosotros nos gusta el vino.
El vino nos gusta a nosotros.
We like wine.

A vosotros os gusta el chocolate.
El chocolate os gusta a vosotros.
You like chocolate.

A nosotras nos gusta el ajo.
El ajo nos gusta a nosotras.
We like garlic.

A ellos les gusta el té.
El té les gusta a ellos.
They like tea.

A ellas les gusta la cerveza.
La cerveza les gusta a ellas.
They like beer.

A ustedes les gusta el actor.
El actor les gusta a ustedes.
You like the actor.

In the Negative

To make these statements in the negative, place *no* before the indirect object. "I don't like boxing" may be translated into Spanish in three ways, as follows:

No me gusta el boxeo.

A mí no me gusta el boxeo.

El boxeo no me gusta a mí.

Not Just in the Present

The verb *gustar* may also appear in other tenses. For instance, take a look at the following sentences. Can you recognize the tense of each one?

Me gustaba el ajedrez.
I used to like chess.

Nos ha gustado viajar a Lima desde pequeños.
We have liked to travel to Lima since we were little.

Te gustará a mi amiga.
You will like my (girl) friend.

Just Saying "No"

As you've seen with *gustar,* the act of negating a positive statement is simply a matter of placing a *no* before the verb. The easiest example is the sentence *No hablo.* (I don't speak.) As you know, however, any language has a multitude of ways to express a single point. This is also the case with saying "no." First, let's review positive and negative words in the following table.

▼ **VOCABULARY: POSITIVES AND NEGATIVES**

Positive	Negative
a veces (sometimes)	*jamás* (never)
algo (something)	*nada* (nothing)
alguien (someone)	*nadie* (no one)
alguna vez, otra vez (sometimes, another time)	*ninguna vez, nunca* (never)
alguno (some)	*ninguno* (none)
o (or)	*ni, ni siquiera* (nor, not even)
sí (yes)	*no* (no)
siempre (always)	*nunca* (never)
también (too)	*tampoco* (neither)

Positive	Negative
todavía (still)	*ya no* (no longer)
todo (all)	*nada* (nothing)
ya (already)	*aún no* (not yet)

Whereas a double negative in English is said to be logically equivalent to a positive statement, it simply confirms the negative in Spanish. For example:

Yo no voy allí nunca.
I never go there. (Literally: I don't go there never.)

Yo no voy a ningún sitio.
I don't go anyplace. (Literally: I don't go to no place.)

Verbs That Act Like *Gustar*

There is a whole group of verbs in Spanish that behave similarly to *gustar*. The simplest example is the verb *disgustar* (to dislike):

Me disgusta viajar.
I dislike to travel.

Te disgusta el café.
You dislike coffee.

Nos disgustan las flores.
We dislike flowers.

Other verbs that should be used in the same "inverted" way as *gustar* and *disgustar* are listed in the following table.

▼ VERBS THAT ACT LIKE *GUSTAR*

agradar	to please
doler	to hurt, to be in pain
encantar	to delight, to charm
faltar	to be lacking
hacer falta	to need
interesar	to interest
parecer	to seem
sobrar	to be left

The following are a few examples of these verbs in action:

Nos agradan los perros, pero no los gatos.
We like dogs but not cats.

Te duele el brazo.
Your arm hurts.

Me encantan las flores.
I love flowers.

No le falta ni dinero ni poder.
He doesn't lack money nor power.

Os hacen falta vuestros padres.
You need your parents.

Nos interesa el fútbol americano.
We are interested in football.

La camisa me parece muy pequeña.
It seems to me that the shirt is too small.

Te sobró comida.
You had food left over.

What Do You Like to Do?

What do you like to do in your free time? What are some hobbies and activities you are interested in? The following section will help you discuss these hobbies and activities in Spanish.

Going Places

As you remember, the verb "to go" in Spanish is *ir*. Use the expression *ir a . . .* ("to go to . . .") with the words and phrases in the following table.

▼ *IR A . . .*

los almacenes	the stores
las carreras de caballo	the horse races
las carreras de coches	the car races
un casino	a casino
una competencia	a competition
un concierto	a concert
las corridas de toro	the running of bulls
las discotecas	the discotheques, clubs
un parque de diversiones	an amusement park
un partido de . . .	a game of . . .
la playa	the beach
visitar a amigos	visit friends
visitar a parientes	visit relatives

A similar construction is *ir de . . .* ("to go . . ."). This construction generally appears with one of the words listed in the following table.

▼ *IR DE . . .*

compras	shopping
excursión	on excursions
pesca	fishing
vacaciones	on vacation
viaje	on a trip
visita	visit

Activities do require you to think of not only who does something and when but also how that activity is described. Some activities are ones that you "play" (*jugar*), and others are ones that you "do" (*hacer*).

Sports-related activities are generally expressed with the verb *hacer* (to do, to make). For instance, *hacer natación* is literally "to do swimming." The following table contains a list of activities that you "do."

▼ *HACER* . . .

aeróbic	aerobics
alpinismo	mountain climbing
artes marciales	martial arts
buceo	scuba diving
ciclismo	cycling
deportes de aventura	extreme sports
ejercicios	exercise
equitación	horseback riding
esquí	skiing
el levantamiento de pesas	weightlifting
navegación	sailing
patinaje	skating
surf	surfing

With *jugar*, things are easier. The idea of "playing" sports is the same in Spanish as in English. For instance, *jugar al ajedrez* means "to play chess." (Remember that when you put *a* and *el* together, they merge into *al*, as in this case, when you use the construction *jugar a* . . . and *el ajedrez*.) For other sports terms used in this construction, see the following table.

▼ *JUGAR A* . . .

el baloncesto, el básquetbol	basketball
el balonvolea, el voleibol	volleyball
el béisbol	baseball
el billar	billiards, pool
los bolos	bowling
las cartas	cards

los dardos	darts
el fútbol	soccer
el fútbol americano	football
el golf	golf
la lotería	the lottery
el póquer	poker
la ruleta	roulette
el solitario	solitaire
el tenis	tennis
el veintiuno	21 (blackjack)

But some of us like more sedentary activities, such as reading. And there is so much to read—just take a look at the following table.

▼ **LEER ...**

biografías	biographies
cuentos	stories, short stories
cuentos de hadas	fairy tales
libros	books
las noticias	the news
novelas de ciencia ficción	science-fiction novels
novelas policíacas	detective novels
novelas románticas	romance novels
periódicos	newspapers
poesía	poems
recetas	recipes
revistas	magazines

CHAPTER 16

Any Questions?

Spanish has various ways for making inquiries, also known as "interrogative statements." You can rely on the intonation (tone of voice), interrogative pronouns and adverbs, subject-verb switch with interrogative intonation patterns, and interrogative tags. Sound difficult? It's not. You can do it!

Listen to the Intonation

Everything you say has a "melody." Within phrases, there are points where your vocal cords are at their most relaxed—when you pause. There are points where your vocal cords are at their most tense—when you convey a specific state of mind. And more often your vocal cords are in a medium state of tension—when you simply wish to convey your thoughts as carried by the words that you have chosen.

In short, intonation (or patterns of inflection) allows you to distinguish a statement from a question or from an exclamation, as follows:

- **Statement:** Intonation patterns associated with statements generally start and end with low inflection that modulates regularly in a medium tension of voice.
- **Question:** Intonation patterns associated with statements turned to questions generally end with high inflection of the voice.

- **Exclamation:** Intonation patterns associated with exclamations follow patterns similar to statements but with sharper contrasted inflection within the phrase or sentence.

Learn Your Interrogatives

Most of the questions you have encountered up to this point have begun with an interrogative pronoun or adverb. These interrogatives generally begin the interrogative phrase and identify the object or person about which there is some doubt. It is important to recognize that these pronouns and adverbs are distinguished in writing with an accent mark.

Interrogatives (which sometimes act like pronouns and other times like adjectives, but don't worry about that) are special in the number of different factors that guide their use. Keep in mind that interrogatives work to fill in the blanks of notions requiring more information to be completely understood. Some of them conjugate according to number (singular or plural), while others don't. The same is true for considerations of gender.

Interrogatives Without Gender or Number

Some interrogatives function without being gender- or number-specific.

▼ INTERROGATIVES WITHOUT GENDER OR NUMBER

¿Cómo?	How?
¿Cuándo?	When?
¿Dónde?	Where?
¿Qué?	What?

¿Cómo está Mauricio?
How is Mauricio?

¿Cuándo será abogado Rafico?
When will Rafico be a lawyer?

¿Dónde está la iglesia?
Where is the church?

¿Qué tenía Gloria en la mano?
What did Gloria have in her hand?

¿Cómo?

Though generally used to ask "how," *¿cómo?* is one of those small words that have various situational uses. In a question, you may use it to ask about the condition of a noun or manner of an action. If you didn't hear what somebody said, you can say *¿Cómo?* In English, it translates to something like "Excuse me?" This word is also used to express surprise and to inquire as to how that surprise came to occur. (You may also use *¿cómo?* to form a rhetorical question.) For examples, take a look at the following questions:

¿Cómo está el tiempo?
How is the weather?

¿Cómo es el clima en Vera Cruz?
How is the climate in Vera Cruz?

¿Cómo le gusta el café?
How does he like his coffee?

¿Cómo debo cocinar el bistec?
How should I cook the steak?

¿Cómo? ¿Qué significa ésto?
Excuse me? What does that mean?

¿Cómo es que están aquí tus hermanos?
How is it that your siblings are here?

¿Cuándo?

The Spanish "when" is much more straightforward. It is used in questions related to time.

¿Cuándo estarán en casa los niños?
When will the children be at home?

¿Cuándo llegaste a casa?
When did you get home?

¿Dónde?

The Spanish "where," though as simple to use as *¿cuándo?*, is interesting in that it often needs help to express a question regarding "place." That is, it is often used with prepositions. For the list of prepositions, as well as some examples, take a look at the following table.

▼ *¿DÓNDE?* IN COMBINATION WITH PREPOSITIONS

Preposition	Question
a (to)	*¿adónde?*
de (from)	*¿de dónde?*
en (in)	*¿en dónde?*
por (by)	*¿por dónde?*

¿Dónde está Gloria?
Where is Gloria?

¿Adónde fue Marco?
Where did Marco go to?

¿De dónde es Marisela?
Where is Marisela from?

¿En dónde se lastimó?
Where did he hurt himself?

¿Por dónde caminó?
By which way did she walk?

¿Qué?

¿Qué? is another word with many meanings. Within a question, it generally translates to "what?" It may:

- Stand on its own as a familiar alternative to *¿cómo?*—for example, to ask "What did you say?"
- Precede a noun where the subject is defined within the question, like "What time is it?"
- Precede a verb where the question refers to something in general terms rather than by a specific instance. It may be assumed that the person making the inquiry possesses no knowledge of the possible responses to his or her question. For example, "What's in here?"

Here are some examples of using *qué* in questions:

¿Qué me dijiste?
What did you say to me?

¿Qué hora es?
What time is it?

¿Qué día es hoy?
What day is it?

¿Qué modelo de coche tiene Pedro?
What car model does Peter have?

¿Qué comida hay?
What food is there?

¿Qué está en la caja?
What is in the box?

¿Qué compraba en el almacén?
What was he purchasing at the store?

Add the preposition *por,* and the result is another question, *¿por qué?* This phrase may be used to ask "by what (reason)," "for what (purpose)," and so on, but most often it simply translates to "why?"

¿Por qué no me dices la verdad?
Why won't you tell me the truth?

¿Por qué vosotros insistís en esperar?
Why do you insist on waiting?

 Essential

When *por qué* is not used as an interrogative, it changes to *porque* (no accent mark) to mean "because." For instance: *¿Por qué no está Juan en casa?* (Why is Juan not at home?) *Porque está en la escuela.* (Because he is at school.)

Some interrogatives do possess *número* (number) but not *género* (gender). Interrogatives that comprise this category are listed in the following table.

▼ **INTERROGATIVES WITH NUMBER BUT WITHOUT GENDER**

Interrogative	English
¿Cuál?	which (singular)
¿Cuáles?	which (plural)
¿Quién?	who (singular)
¿Quiénes?	who (plural)

¿Cuál de los pasteles quiere Marí?
Which of the pastries does Mari want?

¿Cuáles de estos libros prefiere Sebastián?
Which of these books does Sebastian prefer?

¿Quién estuvo en la reunión?
Who was at the gathering/reunion?

¿Quiénes aquí tienen treinta años?
Who here are thirty years old?

¿Cuál? and ¿Cuáles?

Cuál is an interrogative pronoun that causes confusion for many beginners. It may be said that it is the Spanish word for "which." However, you will often see it translated as "what." The cause of the confusion, then, is how to choose between *¿cuál?* and *¿qué?* The rules you should follow are:

1. When preceding a verb, *cuál* refers to a specific instance rather than a general idea. It implicitly presupposes prior knowledge of instances and asks that the respondent make a selection. Compare:

   ¿Qué está en la caja?
   What is in the box?

   ¿Cuál está en la caja?
   Which one is in the box?

   ¿Qué compraba en el almacén?
   What was he purchasing in the store?

   ¿Cuáles compraba en el almacén?
   Which ones was he purchasing at the store?

2. It may establish the selection more explicitly when used within the combination *¿Cuál(es) + de +* (noun/pronoun) . . . ?

¿Cuál de las joyas está en la caja?
Which one of the jewels is in the box?

¿Cuáles de estos videos son buenos?
Which of these videos are good?

3. When used with a form of *ser* and certain words, *cuál* is always chosen instead of *qué*, despite the vagueness that accompanies these words. Here are some examples:

¿Cuál era la diferencia?
What was the difference?

¿Cuáles fueron las dificultades?
What were the difficulties?

¿Cuál ha sido el motivo?
What has been the motive?

¿Cuáles son los problemas?
What are the problems?

¿Cuál será la razón?
What will the reason be?

¿Cuál es la solución?
What is the solution?

¿Quién? and ¿Quiénes?

Quién is much less complicated than most interrogative pronouns. It is translated as "who" or "whom"—all you have to be concerned about is the number of people being represented. Furthermore, keep in mind that *quién* and *quiénes* sometimes appear with a preposition, *a* ("to," or personal preposition), *de* ("of" or "from"), or *en* ("in" or "about"). For some examples, see the following sentences:

¿Quién habló en la recepción?
Who spoke at the reception?

¿Quiénes participaron?
Who participated?

¿A quién buscas?
Who are you looking for?

¿De quién es ese coche?
Whose automobile is that?

¿En quiénes pensaba Joaquín?
About whom was Joaquin thinking?

Interrogatives with Number and Gender

This section includes only one interrogative, *cuánto*. This interrogative is a little tricky in that it can have two very similar meanings, "how much" and "how many," depending on the number, singular or plural, employed. Compare the following sentences:

¿Cuánto dinero tiene Javier?
How much money does Javier have?

¿Cuánta plata tiene Javier?
How much money does Javier have? (colloquial; the literal translation of *plata* is silver)

¿Cuánto cuesta?
How much does it cost?

¿En cuánto está lista?
In how much time will she be ready?

¿Cuántos años tiene Jorge?
How old is Jorge?

¿Cuántas bufandas tiene Beatriz?
How many scarves does Beatriz have?

As you can see, the interrogative *cuánto* acts as an adjective by changing in gender and number according to the noun that it modifies. For example, if you want to ask "how many years?" you take *años* (years) and modify *cuánto* accordingly (*cuántos*).

A with Interrogative Pronouns

A often plays an important role in determining the nature, subject, or object of the information requested. You've seen it translated as "at" and "to." And, as you remember, it may act as a personal particle placed before objects that designate people. Take a look at how *a* behaves with interrogatives in the following sentences:

¿A cómo está la gasolina?
At how much is gasoline?

¿Adónde viaja Ximena?
To where does Ximena travel?

¿A qué se refiere la maestra?
To what is the teacher referring?

¿A qué fiesta irá Benjamín?
To which party will Benjamin go?

¿A quién vio Jaime en el concierto?
Whom did Jaime see at the concert?

¿A cuánto está el agua?
At how much is the water?

¿A cuántos kilómetros está el museo?
At how many kilometers is the museum?

Subject-Verb Switch and Interrogative Tags

You are probably unconsciously very familiar with the subject-verb switch that often occurs in English to transform a statement into a question. For example: "Mary is a teacher" can switch to "Is Mary a teacher?" The same transformations are possible in Spanish.

La cama está contra la pared.
The bed is against the wall.

¿Está la cama contra la pared?
Is the bed against the wall?

Equally as common in English and in Spanish is the addition of a phrase of doubt to a statement, thereby rendering it, for all intents and purposes, a question. For example:

La cama está contra la pared, ¿no?
The bed is against the wall, isn't it?

Paca no trabaja, ¿o sí?
Paca does not work, or does she?

Rodrigo no hace ejercicios, ¿verdad?
Rodrigo doesn't do exercises, right?

Interjections

The exclamatory phrases that are set off by ¡ . . . ! often use three of the accented words that you have already encountered in the capacity of interrogatives: *¡Qué!*, *¡Cuánto!* and *¡Cómo!* (Note that the accent marks are also present in these words when they act as exclamatory expressions.) With these simple words, the exclamatory possibilities are endless.

¡Qué!

Qué is used within a variety of structures that express surprise or strong emotion:

1. *¡Qué + (sustantivo)!* — What a (noun)!
2. *¡Qué + (adjetivo)!* — That's (adjective)! How (adjective)!
3. *¡Qué + (sustantivo) + tan + (adjetivo)!* — What a(n) (adjective) (noun)!
4. *¡Qué + (sustantivo) + más + (adjetivo)!* — What a(n) (adjective) (noun)!
5. *¡Qué + (adverbio)!* — That's (adverb)! How (adverb)!
6. *¡Qué + (adjetivo) + (ser)!* — How (adjective) + (subject pronoun) am/is/are!
7. *¡Qué + (adjetivo) + (ser) + (sustantivo)!* — How (adjective) + (noun) am/is/are!
8. *¡Qué + (adjetivo) + (estar)!* — How (adjective) + (subject pronoun) am/is/are!
9. *¡Qué + (adjetivo) + (estar) + (sustantivo)!* — How (adjective) + (noun) am/is/are!
10. *¡Qué + (adverbio) + (verbo)!* — How (adverb) + (subject pronoun) + (verb)!
11. *¡Qué + (adverbio) + (verbo) + (sustantivo)!* — How (adverb) + (subject pronoun) + (verb) + (noun)!

¡Qué espectáculo!
What a show!

¡Qué maravilloso!
How marvelous!

¡Qué perrito tan simpático!
What a charming puppy!

¡Qué caballo más veloz!
What a fast horse!

¡Qué lejos!
How far!

¡Qué seria es!
How serious she is!

¡Qué rápido es tu coche!
How fast your car is!

¡Qué alegre estoy!
How happy I am!

¡Qué rudo está Ernesto hoy!
How rude Ernest is today!

¡Qué bien baila!
How well he dances!

¡Qué bien baila Lisa!
How well Lisa dances!

¡Cómo! and ¡Cuánto!

The interjections *cómo* and *cuánto* use their own structures to express strong emotion. The possible constructions are as follows:

1. *¡Cómo + (verbo)!*   How + (subject pronoun) + (verb)!
2. *¡Cómo + (verbo) + (sustantivo)!*   How + (noun) + (verb)!
3. *¡Cuánto + (verbo) + (sustantivo)!*   How much + (noun) + (verb)!
4. *¡Cuánto + (sustantivo) + (verbo)!*   How much/many + (verb) + (noun)!

¡Cómo canta!
How she sings!

¡Cómo lloró!
How he cried!

¡Cómo cocina tu mamá!
How your mother cooks!

¡Cómo lloraba el niño!
How the baby was crying!

¡Cuánto habla Juan!
How much Juan talks!

¡Cuánto lloró el niño!
How much the baby cried!

¡Cuánta gente está aquí!
How many people are here!

¡Cuántos gatos tienes!
How many cats you have!

What's Better and What's Best?

As you often have to do in English, there will be times when your descriptions of things will require that you make comparisons between two or more items. Comparisons can be made to show equivalency or difference.

Two equal modifiers may be compared by using the construction *tan + adjetivo/adverbio + como* (as + adjective/adverb + as). For example:

Mi coche es tan rápido como el de Raúl.
My car is as fast as Raul's.

El niño canta tan bien como su hermana.
The boy sings as well as his sister.

Comparison of objects tends to center on quantity. As such, the previous construction may be slightly altered: *tanto* + noun + *como*. For example:

Mi computadora tiene tanta memoria como la tuya.
My computer has as much memory as yours.

The general structure for comparison of unequals uses the adjective qualifier + *que* + noun/adjective/adverb. To show that something is more than another, simply use *más* (more) as the qualifier. For example:

Hay más manzanas que naranjas.
There are more apples than oranges.

Roberto es más bajo que su hermano.
Robert is shorter than his brother.

Ella habla más rápidamente que David.
She speaks more quickly than David.

Likewise, to show that something is less or fewer than something else, simply use *menos* (less, minus) as the qualifier. For example:

Hay menos asientos que personas.
There are fewer seats than people.

El tango es menos popular en España que en Argentina.
Tango is less popular in Spain than in Argentina.

Él hace las cosas menos cuidadosamente que su compañero.
He does things less carefully than his partner.

As you would expect, not all comparisons can be made so simply. Some adjectives and adverbs don't get along with *más* and *menos*. Instead, they are modified into the comparative form (this sometimes also occurs in English: compare "well" and "better"). For some examples, check the following table.

▼ **IRREGULAR COMPARISONS**

Adjective	Comparative Form
bien (well)	*mejor* (better)
bueno (good)	*mejor* (better)
grande (big, large)	*mayor* (larger, older)
joven (young)	*menor* (younger)
mal (badly)	*peor* (worse)
malo (bad)	*peor* (worse)
mucho (much)	*más* (more)
pequeño (small)	*menor* (smaller)
poco (little)	*menos* (less)
viejo (old)	*mayor* (older)

Following are a few examples of how these irregulars are treated in a sentence:

El trabajo de Sandra es bueno, pero el de Susana es mejor.
Sandra's work is good, but Susana's is better.

Jaime es viejo, pero César es mayor.
Jaime is old, but Cesar is older.

Ser pobre es peor que ser feo.
Being poor is worse than being ugly.

 Fact

There are many other expressions that allow comparison, including: *de la misma manera* (in the same way); *igual que* (the same as); *inferior a* (inferior to); *superior a* (superior to); and *parecido a* (similar to).

Superlatives

Often you will need to describe things of an exceptional nature or quality. In English, you would add the ending "–est" to a modifier (adjective or adverb) to describe something that is the best—"biggest," "strongest," "smartest," and so on. This form is known as superlative.

In Spanish, the superlative form also relies on the words *más* and *menos,* which appear with a definite article to signify "most" and "least." The superlative construction works as follows: *artículo definido* + *más/menos* + *adjetivo/adverbio* + *de* (definite article "the" + more/less + adjective/adverb + of). For example:

Supermán es el más poderoso de los superhéroes.
Superman is the most powerful of the superheroes.

Javier es el menos responsable de los hermanos.
Javier is the least responsible of the brothers.

Pepito es el estudiante más vago.
Pepito is the laziest student.

CHAPTER 17

Words for Everyday Life

The only way to really learn another language is to see it, hear it, and think it—just plain live it on a day-to-day basis. The following sections will help you achieve this by concentrating on what most people do in their daily lives, and will introduce you to the concept of the reflexive verbs.

Introducing Reflexive Verbs

There is a class of verbs (appropriately called reflexive verbs) that relies on reflexive pronouns to convey their meanings correctly. Reflexive verbs may be categorized in various ways. Here is a list of words that will help you describe your everyday routine. Try to apply them in sentences that describes what you do daily.

▼ VERBS AND THEIR REFLEXIVE COUNTERPARTS

Verb	Reflexive Verb
acostar (to lay something down)	*acostarse* (to lay down, to go to bed)
afeitar (to shave someone or something)	*afeitarse* (to shave oneself)
bañar (to bathe)	*bañarse* (to bathe oneself)
cepillar (to brush)	*cepillarse* (to brush oneself)
comportar (to involve)	*comportarse* (to behave)
despedir (to see off, to fire)	*despedirse* (to say goodbye)
despertar (to awaken)	*despertarse* (to awaken oneself)

Verb	Reflexive Verb
desvestir (to undress)	*desvestirse* (to undress oneself)
divertir (to amuse)	*divertirse* (to enjoy oneself)
dormir (to sleep)	*dormirse* (to fall asleep)
duchar (to shower)	*ducharse* (to take a shower)
fregar (to scrub, to wash)	*fregarse* (to scrub or wash oneself)
lavar (to wash)	*lavarse* (to wash oneself)
levantar (to lift)	*levantarse* (to get up)
limpiar (to clean)	*limpiarse* (to clean oneself)
llamar (to call)	*llamarse* (to be called, to call oneself)
llevar (to take, to carry)	*llevarse* (to carry oneself)
maquillar (to apply makeup to someone)	*maquillarse* (to apply makeup to oneself)
olvidar (to forget)	*olvidarse* (to forget oneself)
parar (to stand, to stop)	*pararse* (to stop oneself)
peinar (to comb)	*peinarse* (to comb oneself)
pintar (to paint)	*pintarse* (to paint oneself)
poner (to put, to place)	*ponerse* (to put on)
preocupar (to worry)	*preocuparse* (to worry oneself, to get worried)
quemar (to burn)	*quemarse* (to burn oneself)
quitar (to remove, to take away)	*quitarse* (to get rid of, to remove something)
secar (to dry)	*secarse* (to dry oneself off)
sentar (to sit)	*sentarse* (to sit oneself down)
ver (to see)	*verse* (to see oneself, to imagine oneself)
vestir (to wear, dress in)	*vestirse* (to dress oneself)

Do keep in mind that even if you perform an action on a part of yourself (let's say, when you wash your hands or brush your hair), you should still use the reflexive form of the verb (*lavarse las manos, cepillarse el pelo*).

One peculiarity in the way parts of the body are treated in Spanish, particularly with the reflexive verbs, involves not expressing possession. So when you wash your hands, the literal translation of what you say in Spanish is not "I wash my hands," but rather "I wash the hands." Since many of the things you do on a daily basis do involve different parts of your body, first look at the table of reflexive verbs and think about how you might describe your routine. Before actually writing down your routine, however, list the various verbs that describe acts that you can perform on the specific body parts listed. Also, don't forget to learn the definite article of each of the words describing parts of your body—it will help you remember the word's gender.

▼ **THE HUMAN BODY**

Spanish	English	Spanish	English
el antebrazo	forearm	la mejilla	cheek
la axila	armpit	la muela	molar
la barbilla	chin	la muñeca	wrist
la boca	mouth	el músculo	muscle
el brazo	arm	el muslo	thigh
la cabeza	head	la nariz	nose
la cara	face	la oreja	outer ear
la ceja	eyebrow	el pelo	hair
el codo	elbow	la pestaña	eyelash
el cuello	neck	el pie	foot
el dedo	finger	la pierna	leg
el diente	tooth	la planta del pie	sole of foot
la encía	gum	la quijada	jaw
la frente	forehead	la sien	temple
el labio	lip	el talón	heel
la lengua	tongue	el tobillo	ankle
la mano	hand		

The structure of these reflexive constructions is generally simple: subject + reflexive pronoun + verb. Here's an example of how reflexive verbs work:

Lavo los platos.
I wash the plates.

Me lavo las manos.
I wash my hands.

In the first sentence, the action is done by the subject toward *los platos* (the direct object). In the second sentence, the direct object is *las manos,* which is part of *yo,* so the sentence is reflexive—the action is done to one's self.

Additional Categories of Reflexive Verbs

Not all reflexive verbs are concerned with personal hygiene and the daily routine. Some reflexive verbs are categorized by the standardized manner in which they are translated into English. One category includes the verbs that may be translated with the words "to get . . ."

▼ **REFLEXIVE VERBS THAT MEAN "TO GET . . ."**

Verb	Reflexive Verb
acercar (to bring near)	*acercarse* (to get closer)
alegrar (to make happy, to enliven)	*alegrarse* (to get happy)
alistar (to ready, prepare)	*alistarse* (to get ready)
asustar (to frighten)	*asustarse* (to get frightened)
cansar (to make tired)	*cansarse* (to get tired)
callar (to quiet a person or situation)	*callarse* (to get quiet)
emborrachar (to make drunk)	*emborracharse* (to get drunk)
enfermar (to sicken)	*enfermarse* (to get sick)
enfriar (to make cold)	*enfriarse* (to get cold)
entusiasmar (to excite)	*entusiasmarse* (to get enthusiastic, excited)
inquietar (to incite)	*inquietarse* (to get restless)
marear (to make dizzy)	*marearse* (to get dizzy)
mejorar (to make better)	*mejorarse* (to get better)

Another category contains verbs that change meaning radically with the addition of the reflexive pronoun. You really need to learn these pairs separately, since knowing one won't necessarily help you figure out the meaning of the other.

▼ OTHER REFLEXIVE VERBS

Verb	Reflexive Verb
acabar (to finish, to end)	*acabarse* (to run out of, to ruin one's condition)
acordar (to agree)	*acordarse* (to remember)
burlar (to trick)	*burlarse* (to make fun of, to ridicule)
comportar (to involve)	*comportarse* (to behave)
dar (to give)	*darse a* (to devote oneself to)
dar (to give)	*darse con/contra* (to hit oneself with/against)
	darse por (to consider oneself)
enojar (to make angry)	*enojarse* (to become angry)
fiar (to trust, to lend)	*fiarse* (to trust)
fijar (to fix, to fasten)	*fijarse* (to settle in, to notice)
	fijarse a (to pay attention to)
ir (to go someplace)	*irse* (to go away, to leave)
liar (to tie up)	*liarse con alguien* (to have an affair with someone)
llevar (to take, to carry)	*llevarse* (to get, to win)
	llevarse bien/mal (to get along well/poorly)
negar (to deny, to refuse)	*negarse* (to deny oneself)
parecer (to seem)	*parecerse* (to be alike, to look alike)
portar (to carry)	*portarse bien/mal* (to behave oneself/be naughty)
probar (to prove, to test, to try, to taste)	*probarse* (to try on)
quedar (to remain, to stay, to fit, to be left over)	*quedarse con* (to keep)
quemar (to burn)	*quemarse* (to burn oneself out)
quitar (to remove, to take away)	*quitarse* (to go away, to get rid of something)
referir (to tell, to relate)	*referirse* (to refer to)
saltar (to jump)	*saltarse* (to skip, to come off)
sentir (to feel)	*sentirse bien/mal* (to feel well/ill)
reír (to laugh at)	*reírse* (to laugh)

And, finally, there's a category of verbs that can exist only in the reflexive form. Without reflexive pronouns, these verbs don't have any meaning. Refer to the following table for a list of verbs that are always reflexive.

▼ VERBS THAT EXIST ONLY IN THE REFLEXIVE FORM

Spanish	English
arrepentirse	to regret
atenerse	to abide by, to conform, to comply
atreverse	to dare
atreverse con alguien	to be disrespectful with someone
quejarse	to complain
rebelarse	to rebel
resentirse con/contra	to feel resentment toward/against

Constructions with *Ponerse*

One word in particular, *ponerse* (which normally means "to put on," as in clothing), adopts a new meaning ("to start to") when placed in a combination with *a* + infinitive.

▼ *PONERSE + A* + INFINITIVE

Verb	Ponerse + A + Verb
vestir (to dress)	*ponerse a vestir* (to start to dress)
caminar (to walk)	*ponerse a caminar* (to start to walk)
llorar (to cry)	*ponerse a llorar* (to start to cry)
comer (to eat)	*ponerse a comer* (to start to eat)

Your Home

A big part of your life is the place where you spend at least some of your free time, and where your Spanish zone is—your home! *¿Dónde vive?* (Where do you live?) You might live in an apartment (*un apartamento*), a house (*una casa*), or a dormitory (*un dormitorio* or *una residencia de estudiante*). The following vocabulary tables will provide you with some Spanish words related to your home, which you can use to answer questions in the next exercise.

▼ VOCABULARY: IN YOUR HOME

Spanish	English	Spanish	English
el ático	attic	la lavandería	laundry room
el balcón	balcony	el patio	patio
la cocina	kitchen	el piso	level, floor
el comedor	dining room	la sala	living room
el cuarto de baño	bathroom	la sala de estar	family room
el dormitorio	bedroom	el sótano	basement
el garaje	garage	el suelo	floor
el jardín	garden	el techo	roof

▼ VOCABULARY: FURNITURE

Spanish	English
la alfombra	carpet
la almohada	pillow
el armario	closet
el cajón	drawer
la cama	bed
el colchón	mattress
el cuadro	picture
el despertador eléctrico	electric alarm
el espejo	mirror
el estante para libros	bookcase
la lámpara	lamp

▼ VOCABULARY: IN THE KITCHEN

Spanish	English
la batidora	hand mixer
la cafetera eléctrica	electric coffeemaker
el cajón de cubiertos	cutlery drawer
la cocina de gas	gas stove
el congelador	freezer
el escurridor de platos	dish drainer
el estante de las especias	spice rack

Spanish	English
el fregadero	(kitchen) sink
el grifo de agua	water tap
el horno	oven
el lavavajillas	dishwasher
el microondas	microwave
la nevera	refrigerator

Colors

Chances are probably good that most of the things that are in your home are there because they are either functional or pleasing to your eyes. Regardless of function or aesthetics, you probably coordinate much of what you have by color. The colors of the things you choose make you the artist within your home, placing a white toaster here and a blue wastebasket there. Take a look at the following table for some vocabulary you need to start adding color into your descriptions.

▼ VOCABULARY: COLORS

Spanish	English	Spanish	English
amarillo	yellow	morado	purple
anaranjado	orange	negro	black
azul	blue	oscuro	dark
beige	beige	pardo	brown
blanco	white	rojo	red
café	brown	rosado	pink
claro	light	verde	green
gris	gray	violeta	violet
marrón	brown		

Alert

> As adjectives, colors must agree with the gender and number (singular or plural) of the nouns they describe. Colors ending in –e or a consonant cannot be modified by gender; they can only agree with the items they modify in number. For example: *Elisa tiene camisas azules claras.* (Elisa has light blue shirts.)

Dining Out

Dining out for the first time at a Spanish restaurant does not have to be a stressful situation. Don't worry—you don't have to express everything perfectly and in complete sentences. Armed with a smile and a friendly attitude, you should be able to get by on a minimal vocabulary.

Often verbs aren't even needed. Simply read aloud the items you want from *el menú* (the menu) and add a *por favor* (please) at the end of your request. When the food comes, don't forget to say *gracias* (thank you). At the end of the meal, you say *la cuenta, por favor* (check, please). Pay your bill, say *muchas gracias,* and you are out the door. Here are a few other examples that might help you along:

Necesito un poco de mostaza para mi perro caliente.
I need a little bit of mustard for my hot dog.

Yo quiero el bistec poco asado.
I want the steak rare.

Rocío quería vino tinto con su cena.
Rocio wanted red wine with her dinner.

Marcos no quiso conducir después de tomar bebidas alcohólicas.
Marcos did not want to drive after drinking alcoholic beverages.

¿Se puede fumar aquí?
Can one smoke here?

When looking at a menu, you will see so many dining options that it is impossible to present a complete list. But here are some foods that may interest you.

▼ VOCABULARY: MEATS AND SEAFOOD

Spanish	English	Spanish	English
la almeja	clam	el jamón	ham
el atún	tuna	la langosta	lobster
el ave	poultry	el pescado	fish
el bistec	steak	el pollo	chicken
las camarones	shrimp	la salchicha	sausage
la carne de res	beef	el salmón	salmon
el cerdo	pork	la ternera	veal
la chuleta	chop (cut of meat)	el tiburón	shark
el cordero	lamb	el tocino	bacon
el hígado	liver		

 Fact

How well you want something cooked is just a matter of degrees and can be communicated by simply adding *poco* (a little), *casi* (almost), and *bien* (well, colloquial) to one of the previous preparation methods. You can also say *poco hecho* (rare) or *muy hecho* (very or well done). For example: *Quiero el bistec bien asado, pero mi esposa lo quiere casi crudo.* (I want the steak well done, but my wife would like it almost raw.)

▼ VOCABULARY: FRUITS AND VEGETABLES

Spanish	English	Spanish	English
la berenjena	eggplant	la lima	lime
el brócoli	broccoli	el limón	lemon
la cebolla	onion	el mango	mango
la cereza	cherry	la manzana	apple
el champiñón	mushroom	el melón	melon

Spanish	English	Spanish	English
la ciruela	plum	la naranja	orange
el durazno	peach	la papa	potato
las espinacas	spinach	el pepino	cucumber
la fresa	strawberry	la pera	pear
los frijoles	beans	la piña	pineapple
la guayaba	guava	la uva	grape
la lechuga	lettuce	la zanahoria	carrot

▼ VOCABULARY: OTHER FOODS

Spanish	English	Spanish	English
el arroz	rice	la mantequilla	butter
el arroz con leche	rice pudding	la miel	honey
la avena	oats	el pan	bread
el flan	caramel custard	las pasas	raisins
la galleta	cookie	el pastel	cake, pie
los huevos	eggs	el queso	cheese
la leche	milk	el trigo	wheat
el maíz	corn		

In addition to the food itself, you are more than likely to be interested in how the food is prepared. For some relevant vocabulary, see the following table.

▼ VOCABULARY: FOOD PREPARATION

Spanish	English	Spanish	English
ahumado	smoked	crudo	raw
a la parilla	grilled	frito	fried
a la romana	deep-fried	hervido	boiled
asado	roasted	salteado	sautéed

INDEX

We Have
EVERYTHING
on Anything!

The Everything® list spans a wide range of subjects, with more than 500 titles covering 25 different categories:

Business	History	Reference
Careers	Home Improvement	Religion
Children's Storybooks	Everything Kids	Self-Help
Computers	Languages	Sports & Fitness
Cooking	Music	Travel
Crafts and Hobbies	New Age	Wedding
Education/Schools	Parenting	Writing
Games and Puzzles	Personal Finance	
Health	Pets	